HAYNES GREAT CARS

MINI

HAYNES GREAT CARS

MINI

A celebration of Britain's best-loved small car

GRAHAM ROBSON

A catalogue record for this book is available from the British Library

ISBN 1 84425 326 0

Library of Congress catalog card number 2006924142

Published by Haynes Publishing,
Sparkford, Yeovil, Somerset BA22 7JJ, England

Tel: 01963 442030 Fax: 01963 440001
Int. tel: +44 1963 442030 Int. fax: +44 1963 440001
E-mail: sales@haynes.co.uk
Website: www.haynes.co.uk

Haynes North America Inc.
861 Lawrence Drive, Newbury Park, California 91320, USA

Edited by Warren Allport
Designed by Richard Parsons

Printed and bound in Great Britain by J. H. Haynes & Co. Ltd

PHOTOGRAPH CREDITS
Author's collection: 6–9, 11–13, 15 top, 16 top, 17, 18, 20, 29 top, 30, 32 bottom, 34, 42, 44 middle, 46, 47 bottom, 48 except bottom left, 49, 50 bottom, 51, 53 upper pair, 58 bottom, 59, 60, 61 top, 62, 63, 64 top, 69 right pair, 76 top, 79 bottom, 80, 81 bottom, 82–84, 89, 90, 91 top, 92, 94, 96, 114, 116–119, 121, 124, 132, 133 top, 134, 135–137, 138 except middle right, 140, 145 top, 147 bottom, 148, 149, 153, 154–157
BMW Archive: 41, 44 bottom, 47 top, 48 bottom left, 50 top, 52 bottom, 104 top, 144 top, 145 bottom pair, 146 top, 147 top.
British Motor Industry Heritage Trust: 14, 15 bottom, 16 bottom, 19, 21, 22, 24, 25, 28, 35 top, 43, 44 top, 58 upper pair, 61 lower pair, 64 bottom, 66, 67, 69 top left, 74, 75, 76 lower right, 78, 79 top, 81 top, 88, 91 bottom pair, 93, 95, 97, 99, 104 bottom, 105, 108, 110, 111, 113, 120, 131 bottom, 132 top right, 133 bottom right, 138 middle right, 141–143, 144 bottom, 146 bottom, 150, 151
John Colley: 26, 27, 29 bottom, 31, 32 top, 33, 35 bottom trio, 36, 37, 38, 40, 39, 70–73, 76 lower left
LAT Archive: 68
Tom Wood: Jacket, 2–3, 53–57, 98, 100, 101, 86, 87, 102, 103, 106–107, 122–123, 125, 126–130, 133 bottom left

Contents

Introduction

Alec Issigonis's original Mini was one of those cars that changed the face of motoring. Before it arrived there were accepted, conventional, ways of designing a great car – and afterwards there was the Mini way. Within a motoring generation, almost every other car company was copying the layout and reaping the benefits.

Whatever seemed to us as the right way to lay out a car was changed for ever when we saw the Mini. We can now look back on that date in August 1959, when it was unveiled, and see that every accepted standard had suddenly become obsolete. With its transversely mounted engine, its front-wheel drive, and its incredibly compact dimensions, the Mini was surely just as every car should be?

How could it be that we had seen, tried, and approved of so many other ways to design a car – front engine/rear drive, rear engine/rear drive, air-cooled or water-cooled engines – and yet we had never before experienced the magically compact, technically excellent, and incredibly nimble combination of virtues which the Mini provided? Was it really possible that motor cars had been on sale, all round the world, for more than 70 years before the Mini layout appeared?

At the end of the second millennium, when learned pundits sat down to survey the motoring history of the 20th Century, they rapidly concluded that three very different cars had made the most impact. One was Henry Ford's Model T, one was Dr Porsche's VW Beetle – and the third was Alec Issigonis's Mini. Each had been conceived by an engineer who refused to follow a trend but invented a new one. Each had been designed to sell at low prices and to satisfy the masses – and each was intended to sell in large numbers.

Not that the Mini, or its inventor, were perfect. Over the years, no doubt, Issigonis' skills as an automotive engineer have sometimes been overstated – he was, after all, a haughty, single-minded, individual who was unwilling to accept that anyone else's ideas were the equal of his own, he was rather scornful of cost-conscious managers, and he put passenger comfort way down his list of priorities but there is no doubt that his 'One Big Thing' – the Mini – was a magnificent and successful concept of the way that motor cars should be made.

Fate, of course, had much to do with the success of the Mini. If Issigonis's work at Alvis had not been rejected, if he had not gone to work for the British Motor Corporation in the mid-1950s, if the Suez war had not put the supply of oil to the world into jeopardy in 1956, and if BMC's Sir Leonard Lord had not developed such a hatred of Europe's latest economy cars, it might never even have been conceived.

The world, indeed, is lucky that he was encouraged to design the Mini when he did so, for it was only BMC's dynamic Chairman who had the vision, and the executive power, to see that the Mini was approved and put on sale. It was Sir Leonard's faith in his remote, ascetic, and rather arrogant engineer that overrode all his staff's run-of-the-mill objections to his new car.

Purely by chance, it seems, in 1957 at BMC Issigonis was the right man, in the right place, with the right backers, at the right time, to perform an engineering miracle. Not that he invented the Mini without some prodding. Work under way at Longbridge was on different types of motor car and it was only Len Lord's directive that he should design something to 'beat those bloody bubble cars,' which made him sit down and think.

This, then, is the story of one car, its long career, and how it came to change the shape of other cars, all over the world. I have tried not to make it a dry-as-dust record of introduction dates, chassis numbers, and horsepower ratings but to include all the human and economic factors that led it to remain on sale for 41 eventful years.

The story of the Mini, in fact, is complicated: much more about marketing than engineering and much more about dealer and brand politics than about financial economics. Although the Mini's design, layout, roadholding, and character were all peerless, the way in which the brand was supported (or neglected, even) over the years was sometimes quite pitiful.

This, also, is a story that charts the rise and downfall of the British Motor Corporation, the rise and downfall of British Leyland, and the hideously complex story of successor companies, which stumbled on through the 1980s and 1990s.

I hope I have explained why company politics made it necessary for Minis to be assembled on two sites, for Minis to be sold behind so many different marque badges, and why many essential improvements were never made or made decades too late.

Assembly at Cowley ended in 1968 (to make way for the Austin Maxi – a grave mistake, surely?), the Moke was sent off to Australia in the same year, Mini-Coopers, Riley Elf and Wolseley Hornet types were dropped in 1969, and Mini (as a brand) took over from Austin and Morris badged models at the end of 1969 too.

In the first full year (1960) 116,677 Minis of all types would be produced, with no fewer than 318,475 in 1971 (the best year

ever) but annual production dropped below 200,000 in 1978, was 165,502 in 1979, then below 100,000 in 1981, and below 25,000 in 1993. With annual sales fewer than 15,000 a year after the 1996 revamp, Mini assembly was only an indulgence. The end came in October 2000 after only 7,070 cars had been built during that year.

Economists might look at the Mini's career – particularly at the way that it seemed to fall away after the five millionth car was built in 1986 – and suggest that it should have been killed off there and then but, in the end, it never lost its cheeky, lovable, and immediately recognisable reputation. After all, can 5,378,776 owners all be wrong?

Above: Underneath all that glitz, decked out for the Canadian market, is a Mini. But did the little car's cheeky elegance need to be disguised like that?

Left: When stories spread that the Metro would replace the Mini in 1980, the company moved quickly to kill those rumours. In fact the Mini 'stuck around' for another 20 years.

Left: British Leyland chose a Mini Clubman to emphasise that it had built five million front-wheel-drive cars in the early 1970s. Left to right were Alec Issigonis, George Turnbull, Harry Webster and a charming model.

Opposite: Minis were completely classless, and appealed to every type of buyer. To make the point, this is why Austin-Rover posed a mid-1980s 'Mayfair' in a Mayfair apartment in central London.

Acknowledgements

Because this is a book that has been gathering in my mind for at least the past 40 years, it would be impossible for me to list everyone who has helped to make it possible. Since I bought my first Mini in 1960, and first rode in a Mini-Cooper rally car in 1963, there has rarely been a year when some Mini novelty, or kind person connected with that novelty, has not added to my memories.

This time round, though, I particularly want to thank the five private owners who loaned the carefully maintained and restored cars that we used for special studio photography: Alastair and Sue Gray (1960 850 De Luxe), John Parnell (1965 Mini-Cooper 970S), Dave Naylor (1965 Mini Moke), Suzy Kinsman (1978 Mini 1275GT), and Steve Blacker (1990 Rover Cooper). John Colley and Tom Wood both performed miracles in providing so many splendid images of those five cars.

I am grateful to the British Motor Industry Heritage Trust at Gaydon for letting me browse their now-digitalised website for Mini images that I had not seen before. At Gaydon it was Julie Tew, Lynda Clarke, and Richard Brotherton who put up, uncomplaining, with my interference – Richard and Lynda, in particular, who pointed out sources that I thought had not survived.

I also want to thank John Blunsden, who also dug deeply into his photographic files to help fill in the historic gaps.

Now that the Rover Group is no more (the business collapsed in April 2005), it was never going to be easy to get help and information from beyond the grave. By a miracle, though, Kevin Jones, an astute communications expert who had always kept me informed when he worked at Longbridge, provided further information and advice even though he had moved into another life. Ian Elliott, another long-time Longbridge employee and these days a distinguished historian, also gave unstintingly of his time. I will always be grateful to them for that.

Several Mini enthusiasts made it possible for me to locate the best-preserved cars for photography and in particular I want to thank Chris Cheal, Kay Drury, Paul Hancox, Dave Hollis, and Cliff Porter for helping me to find them.

Stuart Turner, Peter Browning, Bill Price, and Basil Wales were always available if I had a query regarding Minis in motor sport. Collectively, we are all amazed that interest in race and rally Minis has never faded and that the interest in archive information continues to grow.

Many other personalities, of course, have helped me over time – as this book has been brewing for so many years – and I want to thank all of them, collectively, for making my task so much easier.

Graham Robson, October 2006

Opposite 'My Name is Michael Caine' – we all know this, of course. Here, the great man, and star of that seminal film The Italian Job, poses with a car he had personally autographed, to raise money for an ITV charity.

Left: In the 1970s and 1980s, many special-edition Minis appeared. This was the fascia of the 1100 Special Edition of 1979. Not many of those survive today.

Design, development, and manufacture

Were you born before 1957? If not, you may not realise just how traditional – old-fashioned, even – and ordinary Britain's cars were at the time? Those were the days when there were fewer than five million cars on our roads, when there wasn't a single inch of motorway in the UK, and when entry-level motoring usually meant buying a new (but 1930s-style) Ford Popular for £444, an Austin A35 for £541 – or purchasing a 'bubble' car.

'Bubble' cars? What were they? There were several of them around: BMW's £390 Isetta, the Heinkel Cabin Cruiser (£399), and the Goggomobil T300 (£495) – all from West Germany – being the most popular. Such cars usually had a front-entry door, two-seats, a noisy motorcycle-derived engine, rear-wheel drive, and very little performance. They were economical though and, in the absence of anything cheaper, they sold briskly. You could, if you insisted, buy a Reliant Regal three-wheeler (£431), or even a Bond Minicar (£304) – but those who did that tended to be trading up from motor cycles and would never have dared to use one to turn up at the golf club. Once, maybe, but never again...

Most British drivers, therefore, settled for A35s, Morris Minor 1000s, or Standard Eights, which cruised at 60mph and probably recorded more than 30mpg. Good, so far – but all had hard suspension, cramped four-seater cabins, and traditional behaviour. However, with petrol still selling at about 25 pence a gallon (6p a litre) – yes, really – and with Austin and Morris dealers in every high street, no one complained.

Except that the first Suez war had just flared up, petrol stocks were sliding, and our Government had imposed petrol rationing: ten gallons (45 litres) a month didn't seem to go very far. Extra excise duty was applied while rationing lasted – and the cynics doubted if it would ever be removed.

Maybe this situation wasn't going to persist for long and maybe the future was as sunny as ever (it was, as it happens, but we didn't know that at the time) – but the buying public panicked. For a short time, car sales faltered, bubble cars became even more fashionable, and British carmakers had to react.

BMC's Chairman, Sir Leonard Lord, knew he must move swiftly. BMC was the biggest carmaker in Britain, had most to lose if its A35/Minor 1000 models stopped selling, and needed smart new economy cars. Its forceful Chairman, who rarely consulted his colleagues before making an instant decision of his own, made his move.

Beating the bubble cars

Alec Issigonis, who had designed the Morris Minor in the mid-1940s, then left Morris to work at Alvis, had returned recently to Longbridge. His very small special-projects team was working with a very broad, unfocused, brief on long-term ideas.

In 1956 Issigonis had started on XC9000, a medium-sized car which (though rear-wheel drive at first) was the genuine ancestor of the BMC 1800: after being re-engineered to front-wheel drive, it became XC9001. Next he turned his attention to XC9002, a smaller car with a transverse-mounted engine and an 'end-on' gearbox:

that car, eventually evolved to become the BMC 1100.

Len Lord was having none of that. Although he had already commissioned a bubble-car study from Charles Griffin's experimental team at Cowley, in March 1957 he swept into the Issigonis conclave (which was close to his own office in 'The Kremlin' administrative building at Longbridge), cornered the brilliant engineer, and succinctly (and probably rudely, for he was that sort of man) told him: 'Drop everything, start again, and build me something tiny to beat the bloody

bubble cars. We must drive them off the streets by designing a proper miniature car.'

Therefore, the XC9003 project was born and shortly afterwards it would be given a mainstream project code – ADO15 – where ADO stood for Austin Drawing Office.

It was almost, but not quite, 'mission impossible'. Issigonis was told to build the smallest possible car but to provide space for four adult passengers. He also knew that this car would have to replace the A35 and, as Lord had already told him: 'You can use any sort of engine you like, just so long as we have it on our present production lines.'

Left: Alec Issigonis's previous masterpiece had been the Morris Minor, a conventional front-engine/rear-wheel-drive car that he had created in the mid-1940s. It made his name – and the Mini which followed would cement his reputation for evermore.

Opposite: The Mini's timeless style was right for the 1960s, and for all the decades which followed. No other car in the world offered so much, in such a small space.

Issigonis insight

Alec Issigonis might not have been a totally practical engineer but he was certainly inventive. If he had not conceived the Mini, then I doubt if anyone else could have done it. Does that mean that he was a genius? According to every lover of the Mini, he certainly was. Anyone credited with re-inventing the entire layout of the motor car deserves that title. Before the Mini, cars were too large, too heavy, or too crude. After the Mini, and the arrival of transversely mounted engines with front-wheel drive, all previous cars were obsolete.

Not that Issigonis was perfect, though he liked to think his products truly were. According to one of his colleagues, the Mini was his 'One Big Thing' – and anyone would be proud about that. Issigonis, on the other hand, rarely changed his mind to accommodate other people. Stubborn, for sure. Arrogant, maybe. Single-minded, definitely? But still a genius?

In 1957 Len Lord might have wanted a new super-economy car but without Alec Issigonis he would never have got a Mini. Instead, Lord might have got a stripped-out, super-bland, update of the A35 – and it would have died young.

Instead, and given a free hand, Issigonis completely re-invented the motor car. If Len Lord wanted super-economy, then he could have it – with a small, light, super-efficient machine. If Lord wanted a full four-seater, then he could have it – but only on Issigonis's terms.

For a deep-thinking engineer – and Issigonis was certainly that – this was engineering heaven. The only 'given' was that he had to use an existing BMC engine – which effectively meant that he had to adopt the A-series – and the rest was up to him. As Rob Golding once wrote about The Great Man: 'Hawk-faced and sensitive-looking with a stooped stance, long fingers and expansive gestures, he is Everyman's image of an eccentric artist.'

Gathering a few – a very few – trusted engineering colleagues around him, he

started work on the new ADO 15 project, at Longbridge, in 1957. Jack Daniels, the chassis and suspensions engineer who had helped Issigonis with the original Minor (and the front-wheel-drive Minor), became the interpreter of Issigonis's legendary freehand sketches, while Chris Kingham, an engine specialist (with him at Alvis in the mid-1950s), worked on the engine/transmission layout. Charles Griffin would run the development programme from workshops at Cowley.

When work began in March 1957, his 'One Big Thing' was already forming in his head. He knew, definitely knew, that old-type traditional engineering – a front engine, driving the rear wheels, with a bulky propshaft tunnel in the bodyshell – would not do this job.

According to Laurence Pomeroy, who co-operated with Issigonis when writing *The Mini Story* in 1964: 'Briefly, he had in mind a box measuring 10 feet x 4 feet x 4 feet of which, looking at it lengthwise, about 6ft. 6in would be available for passengers and about 1ft. 6in for a luggage locker, leaving not more than 2 feet in which to mount the only possible engine. This was the A-series, which measured 3ft. 2in from the radiator to the back face of the gearbox...'

'Mission impossible'? Not quite, for Issigonis had never forgotten the front-wheel-drive Morris Minor (which Jack Daniels used as personal transport at this time!) and the way that with a transverse engine the existing engine bay suddenly looked yawningly empty. Accordingly, to produce the smallest possible four-seater, he took a brave pill, turned the engine sideways, stuck it on top of the transmission, and elected to drive the front wheels. Suddenly, the engine bay could be very compact – wide but short – and his 10ft target looked achievable.

But only just – and only if every microscopic inch could be squeezed out of the packaging of the cabin, suspension, and detailing. Using his famous freehand sketching skills, which were then interpreted by his faithful acolytes, this is what was achieved.

Right: Before Alec Issigonis created the Mini, he thought deeply about the best way to make small cars even smaller. His conclusions, that such cars should have transversely mounted engines and front-wheel drive, set a standard which was followed by almost every serious carmaker in the next generation.

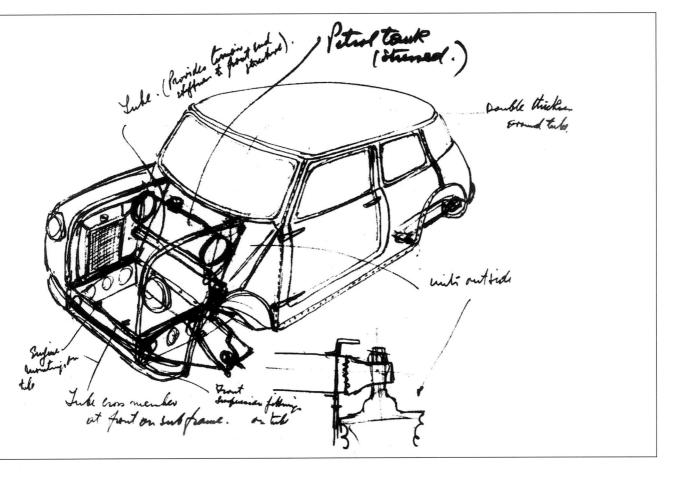

Left: This early Issigonis sketch of the Mini shows that at one stage the radiator would have been mounted on the right (a 180° shift in transverse engine location during testing caused that to be moved) and that he even considered placing the petrol tank up front, behind the engine but ahead of the bulkhead.

A full four-seater

The car, which Issigonis's team rapidly put together, was one of the smallest four-seaters in the world. Not quite the smallest, by the way. Over in Italy, Fiat's Dr Giacosa had already finished development of the Nuova 500, which was only 9ft 8in long. Although this was not a full four-seater and had its noisy little 13bhp/479cc air-cooled engine at the rear, the 500 was a practical machine and would go on to sell in big numbers.

Even so, Issigonis wanted to do a lot better than that. Not only was he determined to build a real four-seater but he would have nothing to do with rear-engined cars. Who was it who once said, of rear-engined cars, that it was 'like throwing an arrow feathers first'? Maybe not Issigonis but I feel sure that he would have approved. Issigonis, therefore, decided to give ADO 15 front-wheel drive.

However, if he needed a length of more than 8ft to package the cabin and the luggage boot, how small could he then make the engine bay?

Incidentally, once the Mini was launched in 1959, BMC produced a cute little promotional film, using simple graphics, showing how Issigonis had evolved the layout. Although it all looked simple, and logical, the truth is that it was not easy – and (even though it was not mentioned in the promotional film) the earlier front-wheel-drive Morris Minor should take some credit.

The huge space-saving secret, by the way, was not just in mounting the engine across the car but arranging to have the transmission under (not alongside) that engine – and choosing the smallest possible wheels, of 10in diameter. Because the gearbox could be tucked away underneath, it meant that the engine could be narrow – and so could the car itself.

Small wheels meant that small tyres could be specified, which meant that small wheel-boxes could do the job, all of which reduced encroachment into the front footwells. Because there was no transmission or propeller shaft under the floor, that pressing could be nearly flat too. All at once, a miracle of packaging opened up.

Given a free hand (except for fierce cost targets, which they missed by a margin), the team also specified all-independent suspension, rack-and-pinion steering, and a seating package which featured a very sit-up-and-beg driving position. Issigonis didn't mind that (he once arrogantly said that 'drivers need to be uncomfortable to stay alert') and he relied on his team to sort out the inevitable problems.

Right: Nicknamed 'Orange Box', this was the very first running prototype of the Mini, which used an Austin A35 radiator grille and a totally removable bonnet/front panel.

Below: The XC9003 full-size mock up was built early in the design/development process in 1957 – still totally 'empty', but giving a good idea of proportions. The front-end grille style would not survive a management viewing.

Prototypes are built

The miracle is not that the job was done, and done very speedily, but that it was done so magnificently. From a standing start at Longbridge in March 1957 with just nine men (but, admittedly, with a free hand except for the engine itself), that team worked up schemes and had a full-size wooden mock-up ready by July. By October 1957 the first two prototypes were on the road and by the summer of 1958 Issigonis thought the project was ready for approval. By chance, it seems, and even though Issigonis had not originally planned it that way, the Mini steered and handled better than any other production car in the world, which was a huge bonus.

Changes, though, were needed along the way. The first prototype cars used 948cc A-series engines, which gave too much performance for what Len Lord and Issigonis required (92mph was talked of – real Mini-Cooper performance before that car had even been invented!) and were mounted with the SU carburettor and the manifolds facing forwards, giving many problems.

At that stage, there was such a rush to complete the engineering that no one thought beyond building stripped-out economy. Door glasses slid laterally, rather than wound down. The parcels shelf was wide and open. The battery was in the boot, under a rubber cover. Floor carpets fitted where they touched (and got wet when rain seeped through floor joints...). The starter button was on the floor, behind the gear lever.

In 1958 no one had even considered making faster versions (Mini-Cooper was three years into the future), nor dressed-up Rileys and Wolseleys. Vans, estate cars, and open-top go-anywhere types would follow but that would all take time. For the moment, BMC planned only to make two near-identical saloons – Austin Sevens (often advertised as 'Se7en' to remind people of the prewar Austin Seven) at Longbridge and Morris Mini-Minors at Cowley. Both those names would be abandoned soon but the car would mature.

Len Lord drove a prototype round Longbridge in July 1958, made one of his famous instant decisions, and directed that it should go into production within 12 months. In fact Len Lord's deputy, George Harriman, and Issigonis may already have jumped the gun: without previously approving a start to the body tooling surely that target could not have been achieved.

Somehow, though, it was achieved. Foreman Albert Green built up the first 'off-tools' car at Longbridge in April 1959 (nowadays we would call it pilot build) and series production began before the end of the summer. The press met the Mini at the Chobham proving ground in August – and the first rave headlines were written.

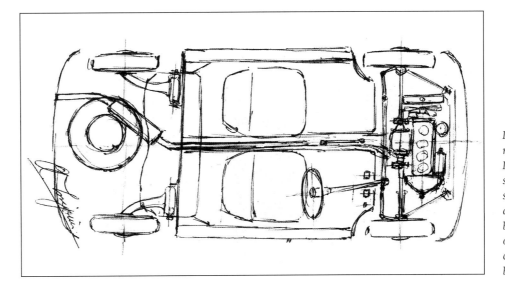

Left: When the Mini was ready for launch, Alec Issigonis took delight in sketching the layout and signing it like the great artist he always longed to be. All the elements are on display, showing how carefully the new car had been packaged.

Engine and transmission

Although Chris Kingham couldn't find space for a gearbox alongside the transverse 34bhp/848cc engine (the front-wheel-drive Minor, a car with a wider track and engine bay, had done that), he found space under the engine itself. This meant lifting the engine by several inches and having the engine and transmission share a common lubricant; neither harmed the integrity of the layout, though many were convinced that such an oil-sharing arrangement would not stand the test of time. Here, as in so many areas, this had never been tried before...

Left: A rare view of the new Mini's transmission, with all gears crammed into a space underneath the engine. This, in every way, was a worm's eye view, with the sump pan removed.

Above: Although the Mini used the existing A-series engine, Issigonis's team squeezed a compact four-speed transmission under it, with the gear-change linkage and casting 'growing' out of the rear of the assembly.

The very first prototypes used 948cc A-series four-cylinder ohv engines, with the carburettor and exhaust manifolds pointing towards the front of the car. After winter testing showed that SU carburettor icing was a problem, the entire engine/transmission assembly was swivelled through 180° (the carburettor and manifolds now pointed towards the

passenger bulkhead) and the radiator swapped sides. An extra idler gear was added to the transmission between the crankshaft and the gearbox mainshaft to make sure that the car still drove forwards (think about it...). The engine, too, was reduced to 848cc, with a new crankshaft that shortened the stroke.

Driving the steered front wheels, through exposed driveshafts, was no problem but providing good, smooth-acting, universal joints nearly broke everyone's hearts. Other front-wheel-drive cars (like the Citroën 2CV, for instance) used UJs which fed back too much reaction to the steering wheels: Issigonis wanted to be rid of all that.

The solution, after much testing, development, and negotiation, was to use a joint first invented by a Czech, Hans Rzeppa, in 1926 and first spotted by Syd Enever, who was Issigonis's opposite number at the MG factory at Abingdon. Originally intended to provide joints for submarine conning tower control gear, they were adapted to the Mini – and Birfield was contracted to build them by the million.

Suspension and steering

Issigonis chose independent suspension at front and rear for many reasons. With no axle beam jumping about at the rear, this could ease the rear-packaging problem. Further, if a modified trailing link system (with no transverse linkage) was engineered it would allow the small boot to be wider and more useful.

But what about springs? Carried away by his 'free-hand' brief, Issigonis rejected the idea of coil springs and conventional dampers and at first thought of using the complex new Hydrolastic system, which his great friend Alex Moulton had evolved. High costs then got in the way, so he reverted to rubber cone springs instead. Conventional telescopic dampers were fitted at front and rear.

The ride, maybe, would be hard (but in the end this helped provide excellent handling) but suspension control was excellent. Hydrolastic, though, was not abandoned but merely sidelined. It would re-appear on the larger, still front-wheel-drive, Austin and Morris 1100s in 1962 and would be fitted to Minis from late 1964.

On the first prototypes there was no front subframe, which eventually had to be added to stiffen up the structure and suspension locations. This increased costs, weight, and complication. Issigonis fought against all these but eventually practical considerations had to take precedence.

Because it had worked so well on Issigonis's earlier masterpiece, the Morris Minor, rack-and-pinion steering was chosen once again. This was extremely space efficient but in this amazingly compact layout it was tucked away behind the engine block, effectively underneath the final drive housing. Generations of race and rally mechanics came to curse this, as changing a bent or damaged rack was difficult and time-consuming...

Left: As penned by Jack Daniels, but as inspired by Alec Issigonis, this was the ultra-compact front suspension/subframe layout of the original Mini, complete with rubber-cone spring suspension units. If only it had been possible, Issigonis would have liked to have done without the subframe...

Wheels, tyres, and brakes

The big advance, though, was to use absolutely tiny pressed-steel wheels – of 10in diameter with 3.5in rim widths. Experience showed that the original wheels were none too robust (early racecars tended to pull them over the wheel studs) but thicker steel gauges soon sorted that out.

For the Mini, Issigonis persuaded Dunlop to develop 10in tyres, which then became the smallest 'real car' tyres – 5.20-10in – in the world. Fiat, incidentally, used 5.20-12in tyres on the Nuova 500, while the A35 had used the more conventional 5.20-13in size.

Drum brakes, 7 x1¼in front and rear, were standard and, although these were adequate to deal with the 75mph performance of original Minis, John Cooper soon found that they faded away badly when he started evolving the car that became the Mini-Cooper. The handbrake lever, naturally, was between the seats and it is often forgotten just how efficient that mechanism actually was. When the car was being used one-up, or two-up, there was so little weight over the rear wheels that a healthy heave on the lever could produce a most satisfying 'handbrake turn', which all owners including the author just loved to demonstrate!

Styling

Although Alec Issigonis liked to say that he did not approve of stylists and styling departments, he made sure that his new baby looked as neat and timeless as possible. It is important, surely, to point out that the final shape of the Mini was strongly influenced by the Nuffield styling department at Cowley and not at all from Longbridge. Except for the use of a different colour range, and unique Austin and Morris grilles and badges, there would be virtually no difference between the Cowley-built and Longbridge-built examples.

Although the Mini was indeed conceived at Longbridge, only a few yards away from Dick Burzi's Austin styling department, the two activities were kept well apart. Moreover, although Sir Leonard Lord had already granted a lucrative styling consultancy to Pininfarina of Turin (the A40 of 1958 would be the first car to show off that link), the Italian concern was not allowed to influence the original shape of the Mini.

Interestingly enough, after the Mini was fully committed, Pinin and Sergio Pininfarina both viewed a car and were asked for comments – which were completely positive: 'Don't change a line' was their ultimate accolade; nor did anyone.

Although this was never to be a car that looked other than totally functional, designers looking for cues could certainly look back to the Morris Oxford of the mid-1950s and see some similarities in terms of headlamp positions and contours. It was a credit to someone's eye for a line – and it cannot all have been Issigonis – that it looked just as suitable in 2000 (but far too small, such had expectations changed in 40 years) as it had in 1957 when originally shaped.

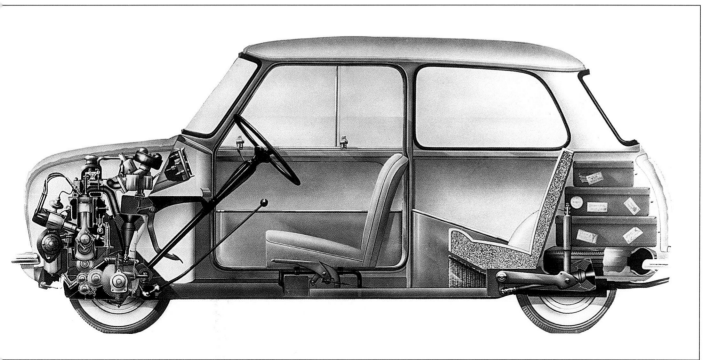

Left: This sectional view of the original 1959-specification Mini shows just how little space was taken up by the engine bay and how more than 8ft of the 10ft overall length was given over to passenger and luggage accommodation. In the next 40 years, this layout never needed to be changed.

Right: Because the Mini was so short, but wide and carefully packaged, its body structure was very sturdy. This stripped-out shell shows the basic two-door engineering, with radiator cooling slots in the left-side wheelarch.

Right: Unmistakable from any angle – this is the shell of a restored Mini. The exposed and angled panel joints connecting the windscreen pillar to the front wheelarch became a Mini signature, which was carried forward to the new-generation machine in 2000.

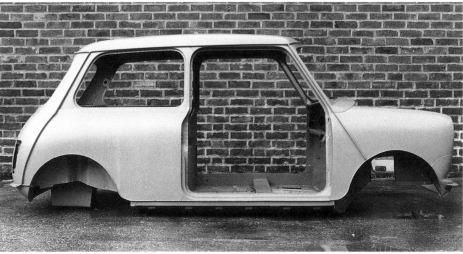

Bodyshell

This was where the pushing and pulling – to save inches, weight, and sheer bulk – was concentrated. No matter how small the cabin should be, Issigonis insisted that it simply had to accommodate four adult passengers. Two factors, no question, which helped make this possible were the tiny wheels (and wheel-box pressings) and the lack of a transmission tunnel.

Because the only sizeable underfloor component linking front to rear was the exhaust system – there was no main gearbox behind the engine, no propeller shaft, and no rear axle, of course – it meant that the floorpan could be

Above: This unusual cutaway display section of the original Mini shows off the amazingly effective packaging.

almost flat. This allowed the rear seat, in particular, to be lower than usual and the roofline was cropped to suit.

Then there were the small wheels. These could be tucked into smaller wheel-boxes. In any small car, with a limited wheelbase, wheel-boxes tend to intrude into the front footwells but in the Mini this problem was limited.

Note that throughout its long life, the Mini never needed to pass a single barrier crash test. Such tests had not even been invented when the car was conceived and, when they did arrive, they only became compulsory for new models. There is little doubt that because of its diminutive nature, the Mini would have failed every

crash test to which it was subjected. As for a Euro NCAP test, shall we say no stars and instant expulsion? However, that was then and this is now...

Not that Issigonis was satisfied. To make the whole car shorter, he pushed the seats forward, then forward some more, making sure that the driving/front seat attitude was much more upright than usual and at the same time pushing the steering wheel forwards, upwards, and steepening its angle.

You didn't like it, right? No, neither did I, but as a space-saver it worked. Issigonis, in any case, didn't care. More length, and therefore more weight, had been carved out of the shell, which was his long-term aim.

Weight fell away in so many other places. The doors had only outer skins and a storage bin, with sliding windows but no drop mechanisms. The heater (optional, not standard, by the way) was exposed. There was only one instrument – a speedometer with fuel gauge inset – and a vast, incredibly useful, parcels shelf on each side.

Front seat adjustment was simple in the extreme – no reclining mechanism, of course, and precious little padding. Rear seat padding, too, was thin – but this gave a lot of scope for stowage under the cushion. Rear quarter windows didn't open at all on early examples. Carpets? Well, there were such things but they

Above: Small car, small luggage boot – there was no way of making the luggage volume any larger. Issigonis's solution was to arrange for the lid to be hinged at the bottom, and to fold back, so that extra boxes could be carried if necessary. In practice that didn't happen very often, as it ruined the little car's handling stability.

Right: Mini assembly getting under way at Cowley – one of two sites chosen by BMC to build the little car – with the traditional type of Morris Oxford taking shape on a parallel line.

were not fastened down and merely dropped into place. They didn't fit very well and soon rumpled up after use.

In the tail, the boot lid could be let down on restraint wires, to carry more bulk. Even so, the spare wheel and the battery (for which there absolutely wasn't enough space up front) were on the floor, covered only by a mat: a hard cover would not follow until the first Mini-Coopers, and other trim upgrades, arrived in 1961.

But it worked – triumphantly and well. When launched, the Mini was 10ft 0¼in long and weighed a mere 1,380lb. The old Austin A35, soon elbowed aside, measured 11ft 5in and weighed 1,484lb. Not only that but the new Mini was faster, more economical, and handled like no passenger car had ever handled before.

Once it sampled the first cars, the world needed no convincing. At a stroke, Issigonis's ADO 15 had changed the face of motoring – for ever.

Building the Mini

When Sir Leonard Lord approved Issigonis's little car in 1958, rebuilding work to accommodate it on two sites – Cowley (Morris) and Longbridge (Austin) – was already going ahead. For production engineers, the use of transverse-installation engine/transmission packaging was one thing but the need to arrange flow-line assembly so that bodyshells dropped down on engine/transmission packages and rear suspension/subframe packages was quite another.

Entire areas of the Cowley and Longbridge assembly buildings, of the Pressed Steel, Fisher & Ludlow, and Longbridge West Works body factories also had to be torn up and re-equipped. At Longbridge, for instance, it was no wonder that the Austin A35 had to be dropped to make way for the Mini, or that supplies of Standard bodyshells at Fisher & Ludlow had to be orphaned.

UK Mini-related project codes, 1957 onwards

Code	Model and dates
XC9003	Original Mini project car of 1957
ADO15	Mini Mk I and MkII (1959–1969)
ADO20	Mini MkIII and Clubman (1969 onwards)
ADO34/35/36	Two-seater open roadster projects (1960)
ADO50	Mini-Cooper and Cooper S (1961)
ADO70	Michelotti-styled coupé (1970)
ADO74	Replacement model but cancelled (1972–1974)
ADO88	Replacement model (pre-dated LC8, which became Metro) (1974)

Even so, it is astonishing to know – to know, not merely to guess – that, although this was the most costly investment programme BMC had so far undertaken, no accurate and detailed calculation of how much it would cost to build the cars appears to have been undertaken. Len Lord, it seems, was far more interested in undercutting Ford Anglia prices than making a sensible profit on the Mini itself – and it was Ford, of all people, which eventually discovered that BMC was actually losing money on the Mini (by buying a car, disassembling it, spot weld by spot weld, and making its own calculations). When Ford politely told BMC's Sir George Harriman about this, he smugly said that he knew what he was doing and that it would all come right in the end: after 1968 and the takeover by Leyland, of course, he finally abandoned that mantra.

Company politics within BMC made it certain that the Mini would originally be assembled on two sites. Seven years after the merger that had joined Austin and Morris together, there was no sign of

Right: BMC's Managing Director, Sir George Harriman (left), and Alec Issigonis admiring one of the very first Austin Se7ens to be completed at Longbridge in 1959.

ationalisation and dealers still competed against each other in every market town.

Right from the start, therefore, BMC planned to make the new car behind two badges and grilles – one to be called Austin Seven, the other to be called Morris Mini-Minor. Austins, it was decided, would be assembled at the Austin factory, at Longbridge, while Morris types would be built at the Nuffield factory at Cowley, near Oxford. The two factories were about 60 miles apart and there was no modern road network connecting them: the M40 and M42 motorways, which now link the plants, would not be completed until the 1990s.

(Not that this policy was ever watertight for, depending on the orders, supply, or industrial relations situation, quite a number of Austins were produced at Cowley and Morris types at Longbridge. In the 1950s and 1960s, after all, BMC had always been like that.)

Because of the huge quantities involved in the mid-1960s, more than 5,000 Minis were being built every week), perhaps this dual sourcing policy made sense, though in some cases there was only ever one source of the major components which went into the cars. In those days (and especially at Cowley) incidentally, up to one third of all new BMC cars were being sent off to overseas territories and factories as CKD (kit) packs – for local final assembly in Australia, South Africa, and other overseas territories was very big business.

Gradually – very gradually – this complicated assembly operation was simplified. As already noted, Cowley assembly ended in 1968, while the last UK-assembled Moke followed at Longbridge during the year. From late 1969 further rationalisation saw the end of the unique-bodied Riley Elf/Wolseley Hornet and the introduction of a common 'Mini' specification, in place of separate and slightly different Austin and Morris types.

Although the long-nose Clubman/1275GT arrived at Longbridge from late 1969, all those bodies were built at West Works. After the Mini-Cooper and Mini-Cooper S models were withdrawn in mid-1971, Longbridge assembly finally settled down – all cars being Minis or Clubman Minis, in saloon, long-nose saloon, estate car, van, and pick-up types.

Above: Longbridge-built Minis always had their own assembly line. Austin A40s are taking shape in the background.

Bodyshell supplies

Because of this dual-sourcing policy, bodyshell monocoques for Cowley-built (Morris) Minis were manufactured by the Pressed Steel Co of Cowley, whose premises were separated from the Cowley assembly plant by a busy main road: an overhead conveyor, with chain-link drive, moved shells from one complex to the other. Although still independent in the late 1950s, Pressed Steel was taken over by BMC in 1965 and soon integrated with Fisher & Ludlow (to form Pressed Steel Fisher).

Longbridge, on the other hand, originally took its Mini saloon shells from two sources – from West Works at Longbridge and from a subsidiary, Fisher and Ludlow of Castle Bromwich, and it was this enterprise that supplied the great variety of different styles that followed in the early 1960s.

Mini bodyshell assembly facilities had also been set up in Longbridge's West Works, which was on the other side of the A38 road from the main car-building plant. From the early 1970s (the facility being erected to help speed up Allegro assembly), the two buildings were connected by an overhead conveyor through which the complete bodyshells were channelled. Until then they had to be transported the short distance from one factory to another in truckloads! Think of the congestion this must have caused...

Originally commissioned for the assembly of Spitfire fighter aircraft during the Second World War, the F & L factory was just 12 miles away from Longbridge, on the north-east edge of Birmingham – so all bodyshell supplies had to be trucked through that teeming city. Many years

Above: Mini bodyshells,
front ends only, being
built at Longbridge in the
early days of this project.

*Opposite: This aerial
shot of Longbridge in
the 1960s, taken from
the east of the complex,
shows the two massive
CABs (Car Assembly
Buildings). The Mini
was originally designed
and developed in the
right-centre of the
complex, facing lawns,
with Len Lord's office in
'The Kremlin' facing
those lawns from the
far (west) side of the
layout. The West Works,
where bodyshells were
built, is out of the
picture to the right.*

after British Leyland had integrated F & L with Pressed Steel, it was hived off to become a supplier to Jaguar, where, in the 2000s, final assembly of Jaguar X-types, S-types, and XK coupés was carried out.

Added to this spider's web of supply was that Pressed Steel also had a massive, modern, pressings-only factory at Swindon (about 25 miles south-west of Oxford), which certainly came to supply major pressings/sub-assemblies both to Cowley and Longbridge: by the 1980s, when Mini assembly was centred only at Longbridge, 60 per cent of a Mini's body was being pressed at Swindon.

Components and assembly

The majority of A-series engines were made at Longbridge, though a proportion was also assembled at the erstwhile 'Morris Engines' factory at Courthouse Green, in Coventry. The complex front-wheel-drive transmission was made both at Longbridge and at Drews Lane, in Birmingham (which was another BMC subsidiary). From 1965 the optional automatic transmission was

always manufactured by Automotive Products (AP) at Leamington Spa, which was about 25 miles from Longbridge.

Although the Longbridge operation was quite efficient – with much of the Mini being manufactured on site or trucked in from nearby suppliers – Cowley found itself out on a limb. Although the bodyshells were supplied by overhead conveyor from the neighbouring Pressed Steel plant, nothing else except trim was actually made there.

Engine/transmission assembly units – up to 400 every day from the mid-1960s – were trucked into the Cowley factory from the Birmingham/Coventry area, as were other bulky supplies such as wheels, tyres, suspension subframes, suspension units, and brakes. There was a constant, and intense, flow of BMC transports up and down the narrow main roads – the A44 from Evesham and the A423 from Coventry in particular – which must have added an absolute fortune in transportation costs to the overheads which the Mini had to meet.

Economically, and in industrial planning terms, this made absolutely no

sense at all but until someone decided to turn the merger of Austin and Nuffield into a sensible amalgamation, it would never be improved. In the mid-1960s, when the Mini was already at its height, nine different families of cars (today we would call them 'platform sharers') were taking shape at Longbridge and six at Cowley, with dual-site manufacture being carried out in most cases.

Although Mini assembly at Cowley continued for some years, it was always confined to the original two-door saloons. Every other derivative – Rileys and Wolseleys, estate cars and vans, short- and long-nose types – was built at Longbridge. Even before the formation of British Leyland (when much rationalisation finally took place), the last Cowley-built Mini was assembled in January 1968.

In both cases, bodyshells were painted and partly trimmed before starting the long assembly process, either in one of the CABs (Car Assembly Buildings) at Longbridge, or in the much-modified/much-modernised final assembly area of Cowley. Separately, and before they met the bodyshells, engines were mated to transmissions, then located in the front subframes, while rear subframes also had their suspension units bolted into place. At a suitable point, the painted/part-trimmed body was lowered on to the correctly spaced subframes, after which assembly continued in the usual, labour-intensive manner.

Once completed and briefly (very briefly because of the daily numbers involved) given a functional test at the end of the lines, the cars were parked up but delivered as soon possible. Even though labour and supply problems meant that neither factory ran even close to its design capacity for long, at its peak in the 1960s well over 10,000 vehicles (Longbridge) or 6,000 vehicles (Cowley) were being finished. BMC had to make sure that new cars were delivered promptly after build, or each site would rapidly clog-up with unsold hardware! No wonder that a large multi-storey car park was built at Longbridge – immediately next to the exit doors to the CABs – just enough to hold a few days' production, in case of problems in arranging for onward delivery.

MINI MKI
1959–1967

1959–1961 Building a new range

So this is where it all began. Pilot cars had been produced at Longbridge and Cowley in April and May 1959, the dealer chain had been alerted, and a few favoured members of the motoring press had been briefed. This is where the Mini phenomenon was born. Soon, astonished drivers would discover just how such a small car could handle so well and could have such an amazingly roomy package. When the sensational front-wheel-drive Mini family was born in August 1959, it set new motoring standards, which the rest of the world's motor industry then spent years scrambling to match.

Some say it has never caught up, for there was something about the Issigonis-inspired Mini package that could never be replicated. Maybe it was the ingenious technical layout, maybe it was the amazing handling, maybe it was the cheeky styling – but probably it was a combination of all these virtues.

Right: Alec Issigonis posing proudly alongside a brand-new Austin Se7en in August 1959, when a bunch of these cars was revealed to the world's press at Chobham.

A favourable reception

The Mini's public launch was at the end of August 1959 and the media gave the new cars a good reception – this almost being assured by the fact that an entire press fleet was distributed among the most high-profile pressmen on a long-term test basis. Perhaps BMC never thought about it at the time but all these cars were registered together at Oxford, carrying a sequence of registration numbers starting with the letters GFC. It wasn't long before some cynic or other suggested that these letters stood for 'Gifts For Correspondents'.

The Mini's two identities

Minis have been around for so long that it's easy to forget just how much the specification has changed over the years. The basic packaging, the miraculous use of space in a 10ft length, the sparkling handling and steering have all been retained – but the equipment and detailing seems to have altered a lot. Way back in August 1959 the first Minis came with two badges – Austin Seven (made at Longbridge) and Morris Mini-Minor (built at Cowley) and, although the two cars were identical in almost every way, Austins and Morrises were sold with different colour ranges, different badging – and through

different dealer chains. As was almost traditional by this time, the grilles were different – the Austin having 'wavy mesh' like the A55, the Morris having a more severely slotted pattern.

It is important to stress the importance of BMC's contemporary parallel-marketing strategy. Those were the days when the group enjoyed up to 40 per cent of the market and there were thousands – probably more than 3,000 – of instances where an Austin dealership would be on one side of a market town's High Street, with a Morris (Nuffield, more likely) agency on the other.

Top right: As launched in August 1959, the original (and some still say, the best) Mini was badged Austin or Morris. This was the Austin Seven De Luxe type, which came complete with opening rear side windows and its own distinct 'wavy line' type of radiator grille.

Below ...And this was the Morris, which was identified only by a different front grille.

Right: BMC was so proud of its very first Mini that it kept it, in the company's Heritage collection, ever afterwards. When Sir Alec Issigonis retired in 1972, he was persuaded to pose by the old car.

What the Mini and its rivals cost in 1959

Make and Model	Basic price	Total UK price with tax
Austin Seven/Morris Mini-Minor	£350	£496 19s 2d
AustinSeven/Morris Mini De Luxe	£378	£537 6s 8d
Citroën 2CV	£398	£564 19s 2d
Fiat 600	£432	£613 2s 0d
Ford Popular 100E	£348	£494 2s 6d
Ford Popular 100E De Luxe	£363	£515 17s 6d
Ford Anglia 105E	£415	£589 0s 11d
Ford Anglia 105E De Luxe	£430	£610 5s 11d
Morris Minor 1000 2-door	£416	£590 9s 2d
Morris Minor 1000 2-door De Luxe	£436	£618 15s 10d
Renault Dauphine	£505	£716 10s 10d
Triumph Herald	£495	£702 7s 6d
Volkswagen Beetle (Basic)	£435	£617 7s 6d
Volkswagen Beetle De Luxe	£505	£716 10s 10d

For a private customer like myself, it made it easy to go window-shopping, to check out different colour schemes, delivery schedules, and part-exchange possibilities. In Coventry I did precisely that in 1960 (when I bought my first Mini-Minor) and in 1962 (when I took delivery of an Austin-badged Super de Luxe). It is interesting to recall that in those days, too, there was no question of a discount being negotiated – the only way to massage the price down was to play hardball over a part-exchange allowance.

Spartan equipment

These new cars were mechanically advanced but originally had very basic trim, equipment, and instrumentation. Technically, nothing in the world could match the ingenious transverse-

Above: Because Alec Issigonis didn't believe in styling for styling's sake, he wrapped the Mini's skin as closely around the seats, cabin, wheels, and powertrain as possible. How many 1950s cars had such a closely shrunk tail around the rear?

engine/gearbox-in-sump layout, the rubber cone all-independent suspension arrangement, that uncannily accurate rack-and-pinion steering, and the cheeky character and handling – but almost every other car could match the trim standards.

I'm not just writing that from the standpoint of today – when all cars have heaters (most even have full air conditioning), wind-up windows, front-wheel disc brakes, ABS, air bags, and radial-ply tyres – but from my own memories of the period and of early-Mini ownership. Those of us who were in the market for a new car – and that included me, for in March 1960 I was ready to trade in a 1958 Austin A35 for a new Mini-Minor – had to learn to understand the thinking behind the radically different Mini.

It wasn't that there was anything missing from the specification – it was

Left: In a miracle of packaging, the Mini's A-series engine was mounted transversely, with the cooling radiator tucked into the nearside inner wheelarch and with all the damp-sensitive electrics, including the distributor, pointing forwards.

Right: On an early-type Mini, where the parcels shelf was open to view, there was no tidy way to stow all one's belongings.

merely that BMC had committed almost all its resources to the forward-looking engineering and that Alec Issigonis didn't really approve of luxury inside a car which he had designed. The equipment might look sparse by today's standards but I was a typical customer who was about to trade from an A35 to a Mini. Both cars had equipment that we would describe as Spartan today but at the time I thought that I was being reasonably well served.

Those were the days when none of us expected a heater as standard equipment, or screen washers, or a radio, or a glovebox, or a full array of instruments. Maybe we weren't happy to pay for them as extras but many of us did just that. On a new Mini, in any case, some items – like the glovebox and the full array of instruments – were simply not available: accessory managers pricked up their ears

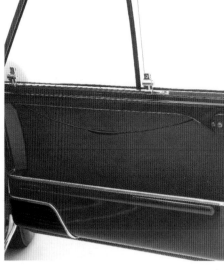

Far left: By using thin seat cushions and squabs, and by using every cubic inch of spare volume, the designers provided much space inside the cabin. Mini owners soon found ways of stowing luggage under the rear seats, as well as in the boxes at each side.

Left: By using sliding side windows instead of the wind-down variety, the Mini provided amazingly useful stowage bins in the doors. For many they were ideal for carrying milk bottles but for Issigonis himself: 'Wine bottles, dear boy, wine bottles...'

...nd looked forward to an after-market ...onanza. In the next few years, an entirely ...ew sub-culture of suppliers would bring ...orward items as diverse as ways to alter ...he rake of the steering column, to add ...riving lamps and reversing lamps, to ...rovide more comfortable seats, extra ...nstruments, different accelerator pedals, ...nd even shaped luggage for the tiny boot.

The lack of basic equipment didn't matter at all – those of us looking for a cheapo-performance car were already bewitched by the front-wheel drive and by the cheeky response, while those who merely wanted a cheap-to-run family car marvelled over the stowage capacity. The Mini, don't forget, may have been only 10ft long but its cabin was roomier than that of the A35, it sat lower

on the road, and it seemed as if there was a use for every cubic inch.

None of us will ever forget those marvellous door bins, which no other car, however expensive, seemed to have on board. If you were a housewife or shopper they swallowed milk bottles, cans of beer if you were a bloke, and bottles of wine if you were Alec Issigonis or similarly trendy. How

...he original Mini – this is a Morris-badged ...Mini-Minor De Luxe – set new standards of space ...tilisation. Although it was only 120 inches long, ...ith an 80-inch wheelbase, the cabin could still ...eat four full-size adults in comfort. As Alec ...ssigonis was once quoted: 'I allowed 102 inches ...or people and baggage but only 18 inches for ...he engine and transmission.'

Right: When the Austin Se7en was launched in 1959, BMC set up this startling publicity shot, insisting that all those people and all that luggage could somehow be stowed into the Mini! Trust me, I'm an advertising man – OK, I suppose it was just possible if the luggage lid was let down at the rear...

Below: If the shape of suitcases was chosen carefully, an astonishing amount of luggage could be stowed in the back of the original Mini.

many of you recall the stowage space under the original rear seats and the way the boot lid could be let down on stays to support more luggage than seemed reasonable? BMC designed wicker baskets to slide under the rear seats but never actually put them on sale through dealerships: private enterprise never truly filled that gap, either.

(Mind you, it helped if the luggage carried on the rear end, with the boot lid dropped down, was light, because a tail-heavy Mini could handle in a most individual manner!...)

BMC, of course, was proud of this stowage ability and published a press shot showing a Mini, in a studio, surrounded by a colossally impressive array of cases, bags, and general carry-on luggage. Cynics suggested that it could not all possibly go into a Mini and still leave space for passengers but BMC insisted that it was so and was ready to prove it. It helped, mind you, that the choice of luggage had been made very carefully.

Trim and variations: the first few years

In the beginning there were two types of Mini – the Basic and the De Luxe, both with 34bhp/848cc power units – this rating never altering in the next eight years. All cars had two-piece sideways-sliding windows in the doors (one of the early faults was that the felt-type seals swelled up in persistent wet weather, which could cause the windows to stick – that certainly happened on my first car) and you operated the interior door locks by pressing down on a cord (this was a real hark back to 1930s sports cars and tourers).

Rear quarter windows (alongside the rear seats) were fixed on Basic models but could be hinged outwards on De Luxe cars to provide a modicum of through-flow ventilation, this being one of the many minor changes which justified the

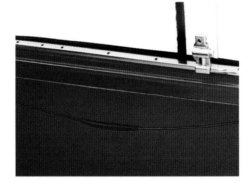

Far left: This was the simple fixing for the sliding window glass of the early generation Minis.

Middle left: To cut down on costs and weight, Alec Issigonis arranged for the inner door release to be by way of a cord inside the doors. Famous traditional-type sports cars had used this sort of release, after all...

Left: On early models, De Luxe types had rear side windows, which could be cranked open by a couple of inches. Although these were adequately burglarproof, they provided a modicum of through-flow ventilation.

rice difference between one type or nother. An original Basic cost £496 19s 2d (£496.97), a De Luxe £537 6s 8d (£537.33) – hat £40 difference probably being worth t least £500 in 2006 money terms. There as a long list of optional extras.

Basic models, in fact, were always quite are. If you find one today, and it is still in riginal trim, it will have no brightwork round wheelarches and sills, tiny 'soup plate' wheel trims, and – most obviously – rubber mats on the floor and single-tone seat upholstery.

De Luxe cars not only got floor carpets (loosely applied, not fixed down – and it wasn't long before they got creased, rucked up and, on many early cars, water soaked due to leaks in the floorpan), two-tone seat covers, and slightly better trim and finishing all round, plus extra wheel

Right: Even on the cheapest Minis, there were recesses at each side of the rear seat cushion, useful for stowing oddments.

Below: Product planning! De Luxe models had these rather fancy types of what were called 'rim embellishers' but on basic models there were only simple little 'soup plates'.

trims around the wheel covers, brightwork around the wheelarches and sills – and windscreen washers.

In both cases, the instrument panel was one single speedometer dial, with a fuel gauge let into the bottom segment: that was all the instrumentation fitted – there being no provision for an ammeter, an oil pressure gauge, or a water temperature gauge. This, in fact, was no more and no less than had been available on the just-obsolete Austin A35.

In a typical piece of Issigonis pragmatism, the starter button was located on the floorpan close to the driver's heels: the heavy-duty cable from

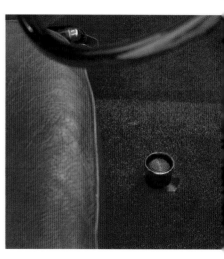

Above: Because the battery was in the boo[t] and cables to the engir[e] were channelled under the floorpan, the start[er] button was ideally pla[ced] on the floor. It would b[e] many years before this feature was abandonec in favour of a key star[t.]

Left: All early-type Min[is] were fitted with a sing[le] centrally mounted instrument pod, which included the speedome[ter,] the fuel contents, and rather dim switchable lights to illuminate the parcels shelf.

Left: If you needed a flashing light to show when the indicators w[ere] in use, what better pla[ce] for it than in the end o[f] the stalk itself?

he boot-mounted battery passed that way, reasoned the design team, so why not locate the button close to it, rather than add weight and complication by mounting it further forward? On the other hand, it was a pity that the gear lever was a long and rather willowy wand, especially since the ousted Austin A35 had been fitted with a slick remote-control change (this being shared, incidentally, with the Morris Minor 1000 and the Austin-Healey Sprite sports car)...

There was provision for a recirculating-air type of heater, a very simple installation, which was mounted on the passenger side of the front

bulkhead. Standard on De Luxe types, it was an optional extra on Basic models: even so, the vast majority of all cars were ordered with the heater fitted. Early Minis tended to leak water around the floorpan and front wheelarch pressings, and the sliding windows were sometimes not quite windproof, so without a heater this could be a very frigid car in the winter: not that the heater was all that efficient...

Although this was a car which handled like no previous road car had ever managed, the driver was certainly not cosseted in his own seat. Front seats naturally had fixed backrests – reclining

front seats were still decades away as far as the Mini was concerned – and although they could be tipped forward to allow access to the rear seat, they had no conventional fore-and-aft adjustment, merely a simple swing linkage that gave limited fore-aft movement.

In his insistence in providing the optimum seating/accommodation package, Alec Issigonis had provided very thin seats, with a rather upright seating position. Because the steering column angle was much more vertical than usual – The Autocar's testers measured it at about 45° – the driver often felt that he was driving a bus – and there was a very

Below: In spite of the Mini's short length, there was plenty of front-seat space, though the driving position was not ideal. Equipment on early cars was simple, to say the least, with only one instrument dial and with open parcels shelves on each side.

long reach to the switches and controls on the facia. Even so, and as with most things in the Mini, we all came to forgive these failings.

Seatbelts, at the time, had not even been considered or provision made, which was probably just as well. When first-generation static (fixed-length) belts were eventually fitted to Minis like these, owners who wore them found that it was absolutely impossible for them to reach those switches…

The boot looked tiny and was tiny. Not only that but its extremities were rather cluttered, for the 5½-gallon fuel tank was tucked in on the left side, the spare wheel was in the base, and the Lucas 12-volt battery was located in a tray on the floor, on the right, covered over by a fibre moulding. On all original cars there was no cover of any type around the fuel tank, while the spare wheel and battery were covered by a loose rubber mat – nothing rigid – which was a very unstable base for stowing heavy and bulky bags. That rubber mat was not robust enough – quite a number of early-specification Minis sometimes found themselves immobilised due to the battery leads being shorted out by inappropriate luggage – yes, it happened to me once!

For the first two years therefore – August 1959 to autumn 1961 – there were four different Mini saloons on sale – Austin and Morris types, in Basic or De Luxe condition. Although only 19,749 cars of all types were produced in 1959,

A great deal of thought went into the layout of the Mini's rear. The boot lid was a large as the structural engineers could allow, the rear window was vast, and the rear wheels were pushed right out to the corners.

Right: To keep down the costs, the spare wheel and fuel tank on original Minis were not partitioned off. The tank remained out in the open, while a rubber mat covered the spare wheel itself.

Far right: Original cars had a very basic tool kit but the jack and wheelbrace provided did a very efficient job.

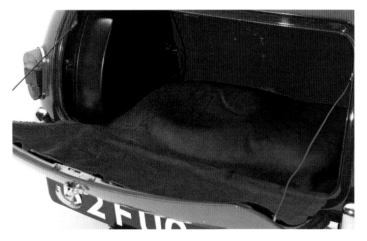

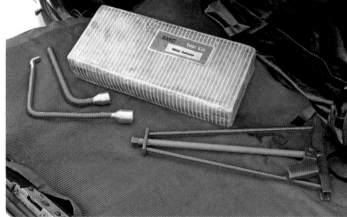

Left: Original-style service documentation for a 1960 Mini.

Far left: Reasons to be cheerful in 1960...were having a brand-new Mini and AA cover. Even at that stage, people thought it important to order one or other of the makes, thinking they were different. This, of course, was a Morris Mini-Minor De Luxe.

Left: Interesting detail on this well-preserved 1960 De Luxe model is the BMC rosette, used as well-liked product identity on BMC cars of the period.

How the Mini and its rivals performed in 1959

Make and model	Top speed	0–60mph	Standing ¼ mile	Fuel consumption	Price inc tax
Austin Seven/Morris Mini-Minor	73mph	26.5sec	23.3sec	40mpg	£537
Fiat 600	58mph	–	27.3sec	49mpg	£613
Ford Popular 100E	68mph	36.4sec	24.4sec	30mpg	£516
Ford Anglia 105E	77mph	29.4sec	23.0sec	36mpg	£610
Morris Minor 1000 2-door	73mph	31.3sec	24.2sec	39mpg	£619
Renault Dauphine	65mph	43.9sec	25.2sec	41mpg	£717
Triumph Herald	70mph	30.4sec	24.3sec	32mpg	£702
Volkswagen Beetle	61mph	–	24.6sec	34mpg	£717

Above: Not much spare space inside the engine bay of the original Mini – but one day there would be twin SUs and a bulky vacuum servo too. Can-opener, anyone?

Right: Not much space to work on an early Mini's single SU carburettor, which was squeezed between the cylinder head and the passenger bulkhead.

demand hit the roof and kept on rising. In 1960 more than 110,000 Minis of all types (including the estate cars and vans described below) would be sold. By 1961 more Minis than any other car were being produced at Cowley and Longbridge, because of BMC's illogical pricing policies, which did little for the group's profitability. The Mini's popularity, therefore, was established speedily, even though some of those early cars suffered from serious teething troubles such as the engine's dislike of ultra-wet conditions (where water spray caused the distributor to start misfiring), floorpans that leaked, door bins that filled up with water after a rainstorm, and from sliding side windows that tended to stick.

Estate cars and vans

Here is a conundrum. More than 400,000 Mini estate cars of all types were built in the 1960s and 1970s but how many of them do you see today? Great little cars, versatile little cars, cute little cars – but as far as I can see, most of them have now gone to that great 'scrapyard in the sky'. Today a good-condition Morris Traveller or Austin Countryman – especially with wood cladding – is a rarity.

Although there weren't any estate car versions when the Mini first appeared, BMC's planners had always slotted them into the 'grand design'. After all, at Longbridge the Mini was replacing the A35, of which more than 140,000 vans and estate cars had been built, so there was never any doubt. The larger Morris Minor Traveller carried on at Cowley. However, because this was BMC and because two completely different dealer chains had to be satisfied, they were always scheduled to be built with Austin and Morris badges.

Although the new Minis were a masterpiece of packaging, making a sensibly useful estate car out of the tiny two-door saloon was not easy – it could so easily have been too short, and too stubby, to make any sense. In the end, the estate cars (and the vans that ran parallel with them) would be nearly 10in longer (and about 110lb heavier) and the load capacity benefited enormously.

Even before the new Mini was launched, therefore, Alec Issigonis's design team had developed a longer-wheelbase version of the new platform, this being used as the basis of three closely related models: the estate cars, the vans, and the pick-ups. In the event, the vans were launched first (in June 1960), the estate cars following three months later. Technically, the two types were close – but not that close.

Although no changes were made to the transverse-engine/front-drive installation, nor to the trailing arm rear suspension, the pressed steel platform's wheelbase was lengthened by 4in. From the nose to the rear of the passenger doors, the style was unchanged: aft of that BMC's stylists developed a chunky and squared-up new box, which could be made as a pure van, or as a smart little estate car.

Inside the body there was one major difference between estate cars and vans – the vans normally had a flat metal floor behind the front seats (this effectively being a flat floor built up over the 'chassis' platform), the estate cars had a bench rear seat.

(Just to confuse the issue, BMC soon offered the rear seat/estate car rear platform as an optional extra inside the vans too – but there were still no side windows. This was a UK-only tax dodge.)

Not only could the rear seat fold down and forwards – the cushion could be hinged forward, the backrest could fold flat – but as there was more rear overhang on this body than on the saloon, this increased the carrying capacity. With the rear seat folded, the platform length was nearly 48in, the minimum loading width was 34in, and the total load space measured 35.3cu ft. BMC quoted a maximum payload capacity of 700lb.

At the rear the estate car's links with the van were quite clear, for instead of a single door there were two half doors – just like the Morris Minor Traveller but different from the Austin A35 Countryman, which had a single side-opening door. Even so, the links with the van did not all appear logical – on the van there was a new fuel tank under the floor, with a filler on the right flank, but for the estate cars (where this would have been logical) the saloon's 'boot-side' tank was retained (behind a trim panel) and the filler cap was on the left...

The nice, retro-feature of these near-identical cars, was that the estate car bodies were clad in polished wood. However, as *The Autocar* confirmed in its description, this was purely for show: 'Polished timber is used at the rear of the body...it does not form part of the structure, being secured by adhesive to the body panels...

'Apart from different radiator grilles, the emblem on the horn button at the centre of the steering wheel and the inscription on the tail, the Austin and Morris versions are identical...'

The names, though, were different – the Austin Seven Countryman (which took its model name from the A35) and the Morris Mini-Traveller (like the Morris Minor 1000 estate) – though the prices, at £439 basic and £623 0s 10d (£623.04) with UK purchase tax, were identical.

All the cars were equipped to De Luxe standards, with screen washers and a heater as standard. Apart from the use of

Below: The Mini Traveller was a very practical little load-carrier, though of course its carrying volume was restricted.

fold-flat rear seats, there were some other nice little touches, including sliding/lockable rear side windows, automatic check stays for the opening rear doors, and a removable rear floor panel over the spare wheel.

In the next 20 years, estate-bodied Minis, vans, and pick-ups of one kind or another, were always in production at Longbridge, all of them using structures pressed and assembled at the ex-Fisher & Ludlow body plant at Castle Bromwich. Nowadays this plant is owned by Ford (for Jaguar's use) and builds Jaguar saloons and coupés.

Below: Standing in the back of a Mini Traveller in 1960, this sheep proves...Well, what does it prove, exactly?!

Right: Because it had a 4in longer wheelbase platform, and a longer tail, the tiny little estate car version of the Mini – known as the Seven Countryman and the Mini-Minor Traveller, depending on the badge – always sold well. The 'Olde Englishe Woode' feature was not essential for structural rigidity but was a styling throwback to earlier BMC styles like the Morris Minor Traveller.

How the estate car performed

No one seemed to know much about drag coefficients in those days – at least they were rarely mentioned – for the square-backed estate car clearly didn't work as well as the saloon. *The Autocar* published its road test in the 23 September 1960 issue and recorded that the test car (Morris-badged, by the way) only reached 67mph, took 21.1sec for 0–50mph, and needed 33.8sec to reach 60mph – on the other hand it recorded 38.4mpg overall.

Because this was a load-carrying machine – the quoted payload was 700lb – the acceleration figures were also taken with a full load, this producing a very turgid 0–50mph time of 24.4sec: 0–60mph was not even recorded in this state!

However, as the testers summarised: 'Already holding a reputation of being a great little car, this latest version will certainly enhance this assessment. For town use it remains easy to park, and is fast through traffic because of its compact dimensions...'

Mini vans: more than just load carriers

How many owned a Mini van before they bought a car? How many converted it into an 'estate car' with side windows but didn't tell the authorities? How many slept in it, instead of using a tent, when they went to their first rock concert? A surprising number, I reckon.

Mini vans and pick-ups, too, were always part of BMC Chairman Sir Leonard Lord's long-term strategy for the Mini. Previous generation BMC LCVs (Light Commercial Vehicles) – the Austin A35 and Morris Minor derivatives – had been successful commercially and he wanted to repeat the trick.

Perhaps they weren't glamorous, and perhaps they weren't the fastest cars on the road, but they suited a lot of people and had many uses. Look at the figures, and the major customers, if you're still not convinced: vans and pick-ups would be built for more than 20 years, nearly 580,000 being produced in that period. Fleets were sold to the AA, the RAC, the Post Office, and the police.

As already noted, the longer-wheelbase version of the 'chassis' platform was always meant to be the basis of three new derivatives: the four-seater estate car, the van, and the pick-up. Commercially, it was certainly justified. More than 210,000 of the gawky Austin A30/A35 vans and more than 325,000 Morris Minor LCVs told their own marketing story – they were cheap to build and very profitable.

This time around, it wasn't as easy as it looked. Many new pressings were needed in the lengthened platform and rear quarters, especially in the pick-up version, which had to have a unique rear panel and window wrapped around the front seats and, of course, a unique tailgate.

To look after the load-carrying role, there were longer rear dampers and higher turrets, stiffened-up suspension and, in the unloaded condition, there was a little more ride height at the rear. There was a second steel floor all the way to the tail doors (or drop-down tailgate, in the case of the pick-up), with the spare wheel, battery, and fuel tank out of sight. The filler cap was recessed into the ffside rear quarter, this feature not being hared on the estate cars whose filler was n the nearside.

Although it was the smallest van on he British market – both in size and in arrying capacity – there was a brisk emand. The maximum load space was nly 55in long and 53¾in wide: BMC uoted a maximum payload of only 560lb this was less than the 700lb that would e quoted for the estate cars).

Style and equipment of these LCVs were ery basic. At the nose of the car, Austin nd Morris versions both wore a painted, tamped, grille while there were expanses f painted metal inside the cockpit. Twin xterior wing mirrors were standard but n interior rear view mirror was not upplied. Incidentally, there was an Austin A35-type opening vent in the roof, this lso becoming an essential fitment on the lamorous 'works' Austin-Healey 3000 ally cars! Vans and later pick-ups had rear quarter bumpers, though earlier pick-ups ad full bumpers.

Speed or legality? – a dilemma

For the private motorist there were snags o be overcome when buying a van or a ick-up (like a maximum legal speed of 40mph!). This was elegantly summed up by writer/Issigonis consultant Laurence omeroy, who commented that: 'Her Majesty's Ministers, in their collective wisdom, had decided that vans, being ousiness equipment, should not be ourdened with purchase tax, and this gave the opportunity of obtaining a vehicle which would exceed 70mph, have all-ndependent suspension, superb steering, and comfortable seats for £360. An opportunity not to be missed! It is true that until the opening of the M1 motorway such a speed was more than 40mph above that legally allowed, and that rear visibility was limited by the misfortune that side windows would immediately attract purchase tax, as well as the cost of putting them in...'

Not that most buyers seemed to care and thumbed their noses at authority, for those were the days when British police seemed to take a liberal attitude, just so

that the traffic could keep moving. In later years, of course, that law was modified and all speed limits were raised.

BMC soon bowed to popular demand and marketed a conversion kit to turn the van into a four-seater (without side windows!) for a mere £15: actually this used parts from the estate car, whose floor and rear seat were structurally identical, though it meant wholesale changes to the packaging of the van's battery and spare wheel positioning.

The fact is that these vehicles, though developed as commercial vehicles, handled just as well as the saloons and were just as cheap to run. Agreed, they were even noisier and (in winter) colder and draughtier but most customers could forgive them anything because of the low selling prices.

In fact the pick-up would never sell as well as the van (without the back-up of van and estate sales such a product would not have been economically viable on its own) but the van would go on selling well until the early 1980s.

Mini 850s in motor sport

In the early days, few people thought the original Mini would be successful in motor sport. Clearly, it was too slow to be an outright winner and although its handling was quite superb, this could not make up for the lack of power. Early cars soon appeared in British rallies, where their handling and traction sometimes helped make up for the low-70s top speed, but clearly they couldn't cope with high mountain passes or with flat-out circuit racing.

Not that the 'works' motor sport department at Abingdon was really interested in the new car. As team manager Marcus Chambers later noted in the book *BMC Competitions Department Secrets*: 'A Mini 850 was delivered...It stayed in the car park for several days, nobody rushed to drive it. Indeed, Dougie Watts recalled that one lunchtime he needed to pop into town, and looked around for a car. Dougie walked over to the Mini...and then changed his mind. He took a Healey instead...'

Even so, BMC's sales departments urged Abingdon to develop 'works' cars, which,

Above: BMC got around British Customs and Excise regulations by making a rear seat optional in the back of a Mini van. Not that the passengers could see anything out of the side when they sat there...

though reluctantly at first, they duly did. Although the new-fangled front-wheel-drive transmissions proved to be infuriatingly weak after the engines had been power tuned, the frailty of the original-specification steel wheels was an unexpected hazard.

Because FIA Homologation rules meant that the single-SU carburettor and cast manifolds had to be retained, even though Weslake (and later Don Moore) modified heads were employed, it was difficult to extract much more than 50bhp from the engine but this was often enough to chew up oil seals and clutches. With tiny Dunlop racing tyres fitted to standard wheels on race circuits,

it was soon obvious that the front wheels would crack up around the studs and this duly happened in full view of the public in the 750 Motor Club's Six Hour Relay race!

The first 'works' rally entry was by Marcus Chambers (a large man in a small car!) in the Norwegian Viking Rally, where it finished 51st, while the first home win was by Pat Moss/Stuart in the Knowldale CC Mini Miglia Rally, and it took time even to gain class wins at International level.

There was no success on any of the

first rally entries – 1959 RAC or Portugal, 1960 Monte Carlo, Geneva, Tulip, or Acropolis – mainly because the little Minis were quite outpaced by the 'works' Saab 96s. Tom Gold then broke the ice with a plucky class win in the 1960 French Alpine (high passes and all...), while in November David Seigle-Morris and Mike Sutcliffe finished sixth and eighth overall in the RAC Rally. That, though, was almost the height of it, for in 1961 there was only one more class victory (by Peter Riley, in the Tulip Rally) to add to the score.

Although Abingdon gave no direct 'works' sponsorship to the original Mini 850 racecars, there was definite support, technical advice, and the supply of engine tuning parts and the latest heavy-duty chassis components to those privateers who wished to race.

Although it was quite unexpected, Sir John Whitmore used his own ex-works 850 to win the BRSCC British Saloon Car Championship outright in 1961 – not by winning races but by consistently winning the 1-litre capacity class and using the marking systems to his best advantage. It was at this time that the legendary Whitmore sideways driving technique was first seen.

All this, of course, was small beer compared with what was to follow. When the Mini-Cooper arrived, Abingdon's interest in the little front-wheel-drive car perked up considerably.

Time for change

Two years after this revolutionary new model had been launched, no fewer than eight different derivatives were already on sale. Both Austin and Morris dealers were able to sell Basic and De Luxe saloons, three-door estate cars, and vans. In the autumn of 1961, however, all that was to change. By the end of the year, with more than 3,000 cars being produced every week in the factories at Longbridge and Cowley, that list of eight derivatives would have risen to 14.

Specifications: Original Austin Seven/Morris Mini-Minor

ENGINE

Description
In-line four-cylinder with cast iron block and cylinder head. Chain-driven camshaft in block, pushrod-operated overhead valves. Heart-shaped combustion chambers. Aluminium alloy pistons, forged steel connecting rods. Three-bearing counterweighted crankshaft

Capacity
848cc (51.8cu in)

Bore and stroke
62.94mm x 68.26mm (2.48in x 2.69in)

Compression ratio
8.3:1

Maximum power
34bhp @ 5,500rpm

Maximum torque
44lb ft (59Nm) @ 2,900rpm

Carburettor
Single 1¼in SU HS2

TRANSMISSION

Gearbox
Four-speed with synchromesh on top three gears

Ratios

1st	3.627:1
2nd	2.171:1
3rd	1.458:1
Top	1.000:1
Reverse	3.627:1

Clutch
Borg and Beck, 7¼in

Final drive
Helical spur gears, ratio: 3.765:1

BRAKES

Front
Lockheed drum, 7in x 1¼in

Rear
Lockheed drum, 7in x 1¼in

Operation
Lockheed hydraulic

Handbrake
Lever, with cable linkage to rear drums

SUSPENSION

Front
Independent, rubber cone springs, double wishbones, telescopic dampers

Rear
Independent, rubber cone springs, trailing arms, telescopic dampers

STEERING

Type
Rack and pinion

Number of turns lock to lock
2¾

Turning circle
32ft 0in (9.75m) approx, between kerbs

Steering wheel
Two-spoke, 15¾in diameter

WHEELS AND TYRES
3½J x 10in steel disc wheels

Tyres
5.20-10in cross-ply

PERFORMANCE
The Autocar road test, Morris Mini-Minor, 28 August 1959

Top speed
75mph (120kph)

Acceleration

0–30mph (48kph)	6.2sec
0–50mph (80kph)	16.9sec
0–60mph (96kph)	26.5sec
Standing quarter mile (402m)	23.3sec

Overall fuel consumption
40.1mpg (7.0l/100km)

DIMENSIONS

Length
10ft 0¼in (3,054mm)

Width
4ft 7in (1,397mm)

Height
4ft 5in (1,346mm)

Wheelbase
6ft 8½in (2,036mm)

Track
Front: 3ft 11⅞in (1,203mm)
Rear: 3ft 9⅞in (1,165mm)

Ground Clearance
6in (152mm)

Weight
1,380lb (626kg)

1961–1964
Cooper, Cooper S, Riley Elf, and Wolseley Hornet

Who was it who once said that every Mini enthusiast should be made to sit an exam paper about the life and times of the Mini-Cooper? And that if they failed to get an A-grade, they should feel disgraced? Not fair really – for although the Mini-Cooper is well known, there are a few oddities to remember in a distinguished career.

This story starts with racing driver/constructor John Cooper, who was a long-time friend of Mini-designer Alec Issigonis. When Cooper had been racing 500s, Issigonis had been racing the Lightweight Special. Both were engineer/designers but in totally different ways – Issigonis was the boffin, the compulsive sketcher, the forward thinker, while Cooper was the practical mechanic, the 'let's draw some lines on the workshop floor' type of designer. Both were hugely successful.

As soon as he got his hands on an original Mini, John Cooper started looking for ways to make it quicker, even though Alec Issigonis, on the other hand, did not really approve of high-performance versions. Cooper thought he knew ways of making the Mini faster – and competitive in motor sport.

Right: Successful racing car constructor John Cooper took one look at the original Mini and decided that he could make a quicker car of it. It was his inspiration, and racing ambitions, which led to the birth of the Mini-Cooper tradition in 1961.

Cooper origins

The very first prototype Mini-Cooper was built in the Cooper Car Co Ltd's workshops in Surbiton, where Cooper found ways to enlarge the engine, fit it with twin SU carburettors, and even persuaded Lockheed to produce tiny disc brakes to fit inside the 10in front wheels.

John Cooper wanted to see the little car in motor racing but could get no support from Issigonis, who resisted the very idea. Nothing daunted, he went over Issigonis's head, approaching BMC's boss, George Harriman, direct and getting approval for a minimum production run of 1,000 cars –

sufficient to gain sporting homologation. The legend is that production was originally planned for a mere 25 cars a week and that many of the BMC sales force thought it couldn't possibly sell 1,000 cars!

Once overruled by George Harriman, the BMC design team took the Mini-Cooper project to their hearts. Development corners were cut rapidly – for although much of the original 850 Mini design was carried forward, unchanged, much work was still needed to finalise the disc brakes (these were the smallest ever tackled by Lockheed) and an uprated engine.

Mini-Cooper on sale

The first ten hand-built cars were tried by the motoring press in July 1961 and the cars met their public in September. Naturally – for this was BMC, with badge-engineering at its height – near-identical Austin and Morris versions were marketed.

John Cooper persuaded BMC to develop a 1-litre version of the A-series engine – that being a convenient competition capacity class limit. To do this speedily, yet not spend a fortune on tooling, BMC

adopted the long stroke crankshaft dimension already being developed for the 1100 models (which were due for launch a year later) and matched it to a new and slightly narrower cylinder bore. This was the comparison:

850 Mini	848cc, 62.9mm bore x 68.3mm stroke
997 Mini-Cooper	997cc, 62.43mm bore x 81.28mm stroke

When this new size was matched to a better-breathing cylinder head, twin semi-downdraught SU HS2 carburettors, a three-branch tubular exhaust system, and a more enterprising camshaft grind, the engine produced 55bhp at 6,000rpm – which, compared with the standard 850, was a 62 per cent gain from only 18 per cent larger capacity. Not only that but these cars were fitted with a sturdy new remote-control gear change – a great advance on the willowy 'wand' of the first 850s.

At a time when Mini 850 prices started at £512, the first Mini-Coopers were launched at £679. For this extra £167 – a lot of money, so many years ago – a Mini-Cooper buyer also got duotone paintwork (red with a white roof or green with a white roof were the most popular choices), a different front grille (11 slats on the Austin, seven wider slats on the Morris), extra 'bumperettes' at the corners, more sound deadening to reduce the clamour of the high-revving engine inside the cabin, and a new centrally-mounted instrument binnacle with speedometer, oil pressure gauge, and water temperature gauge. In the boot, there was a platform over the spare wheel and battery – that was a valuable detail which many 850 Mini owners soon adopted by visiting BMC spare parts counters. On the other hand, the seats were still hard and upright, the door glasses still slid rather than wound down, and there was no rev counter. No rev counter on a

Above: This publicity shot confirms the message that John Cooper was not only a successful racecar designer but had inspired the birth of the Mini-Cooper road car too.

Left: In 1961, Mini enthusiasts found it easy enough to pick out the Mini-Cooper from the original 850 – not only by the new-type grilles and two-tone colour schemes but also by the immediate boost in performance!

Right: When BMC launched the Mini-Cooper in 1961, it made sure that both Austin- and Morris-badged versions were available, though both types were always assembled at Longbridge. This was the Morris.

Below: The Austin Mini-Cooper had this type of front grille but shared the 55bhp/997cc engine with its Morris relative.

high-revving car intended for motor sport. Clearly, the Mini 'bolt-on-goodies' industry was going to have a busy time...

Once the public discovered that the first Mini-Coopers could beat 85mph (many could nudge 90mph when run-in and only mildly tweaked), they queued up to buy and the laughable 1,000 sales target was soon left far behind. Maybe the disc brakes sometimes promised more than they could deliver, and maybe the engine felt rather frantic when pushed hard, but nobody complained – much. Once the Mini-Cooper started winning in races and rallying, John Cooper's original vision was confirmed.

Although 997cc-engined cars were in production for little more than two years, they sold extremely briskly – 14,000 in 1962 alone. Baulk-ring synchromesh transmissions were standardised from mid-1962 but there were few other changes.

Left: Confirming the racecar connection, this Austin Mini-Cooper is posed in the pits at a race circuit, with racing driver Bruce McLaren (in helmet) looking on.

Above: Just for fun, it seems, BMC built a twin-engined Mini-Cooper – one engine in the normal position, driving the front wheels, and one in the rear, driving the rear wheels. As a potential 'free-formula' racing car it had charm but consider the problems of having totally separate transmissions and twin gear levers linked together alongside the driver!

998cc: tiny, or big, difference?

From January 1964, and with very little fuss, Mini-Coopers started being built with a 998cc instead of a 997cc engine. Peak power was unchanged, and there were minor torque improvements, but it was almost impossible to spot one engine from the other just by opening the bonnet and there were no badging nuances to flag up the change.

Internally, even so, there were several important engine changes, which made this into an even more desirable little car. The Cooper's 997cc engine had always been unique (that engine size was never used in any other BMC production car), whereas the later 998cc engine would become a standard A-series dimension, to be used in many other models and produced in millions. These were the dimensional differences:

997cc	62.4mm bore	
	x 81.3mm stroke	
998cc	64.6mm bore	
	x 76.2mm stroke	

The revised engine, therefore, featured a wider bore and a shorter stroke, which meant that it felt smoother when revved hard and could theoretically breathe that important bit deeper. The stroke of the new engine – 76.2mm – translates more prosaically into 3.00in and, of course, was the original stroke of the A-series engine, when it appeared as an 803cc power unit for the Austin A30 in 1951.

Left: In the 1960s some surprising little 'specials' were developed around the Mini-Cooper engine and transmission. This was the Unipower GT, in which the engine/transmission assembly was behind the seats, driving the rear wheels.

Magazine road tests showed that 998cc cars were that important bit faster than 997cc types, which indicates that there was, indeed, more power and torque than before, even though official figures did not back this up. Does this mean that the original claim of 55bhp for the 997cc engine was optimistic, or that the later claim of 55bhp for the 998cc engine was too modest? No one ever admitted to anything but I suspect that the 997cc engine was not quite as lusty, in standard form, as claimed...

By this time, in fact, the Mini-Cooper S had arrived on the scene and the launch of the very special little 970S was imminent, so BMC was about to lose all further interest in the original Mini-Cooper for competition purposes. BMC's sales force, however, was now full of enthusiasm for the little car and wanted it to be as smooth and refined as possible. Thus re-engineered, the 998cc Mini-Cooper stayed in production for almost six further years, selling strongly throughout that time. Radial-ply 145-10in tyres were standardised in March 1964 but, along the way, many development changes were made; these are described in the next section.

Below: Ernest Marples MP, the politician who was also Minister of Transport in the early 1960s, ordered this special one-off hatchback version of the Mini-Cooper S. Although it was a very practical machine, BMC did not take the hint and never put such a car into production.

Mini-Cooper S: the ultimate performance Mini

The cream, they say, always rises to the surface. Maybe this explains why more than five million Minis were made, yet the vast majority of enthusiasts' cars seem to be Cooper S models of one type or another.

That's reasonable, of course, for it was the Cooper S which made most of the headlines in the 1960s, winning the Monte Carlo Rally several times, becoming a crowd-pleasing saloon car racer, and being one of the fastest ways of getting round our crowded towns and cities.

Even so, remember this: of all the Minis ever made, less than one per cent of them were Cooper S types. Even if it wasn't such

a great driver's car, that single statistic would ensure the Cooper S's 'classic' status. Most of the original cars seem to have survived – and many more have since been created from parts.

If it took time to persuade BMC's management that the 997cc Mini-Cooper would sell, it took even longer to convince it that a trio of extra-special Cooper S models should then be developed. By this time, though, it wasn't only racing car constructor John Cooper but his rival Ken Tyrrell, along with BMC Competitions Manager Stuart Turner, who were screaming for BMC to produce yet more powerful engines.

Right: Although BMC's Sir George Harriman was not originally sure that the Mini-Cooper would sell, the reputation soon built up and the car was a huge marketing success. Here Paddy Hopkirk (left) and Henry Liddon pose with the 1071S in which they won the 1964 Monte Carlo Rally.

With more power, this trio urged, not only could Mini-Coopers be better racing saloons but Formula Junior cars using a 1.0-litre version of the engine would also be quicker. However, before such cars could be used in motor sport, 1,000 cars would have to be produced for homologation purposes – the quicker, the better.

By this time, apparently, Alec Issigonis had come to approve of the use of Minis in motor sport: the favourable publicity it brought his product was appealing. With BMC's engine tuning genius Eddie Maher and Downton's Daniel Richmond all lobbying as hard as possible, approval came during 1962. In little more than a year, the very first Mini-Cooper S road car, the 1071S, went on sale.

Most of the technical differences between the Mini-Cooper and the Mini-Cooper S were confined to the engines at first, though the front disc brakes were also enlarged and thickened, making them 80 per cent more resistant to fade and damage.

As everyone surely knows, three types of Mini-Cooper S – 970S, 1071S, and 1275S – were eventually put on sale, each for different reasons. In 1962 the medium-term strategy was to develop special 1.0-litre and 1.3-litre engines – but the 1.1-litre unit came first.

Right: Mini-Cooper and Mini-Cooper S types had a neatly packaged twin-SU-carburettor installation: the chromed air cleaner box on this restored and much-modified engine was not a standard fitment.

Special engines

In later years, the 1,275cc engine became a standard size used in all modern Minis: millions more were made in the 1970s and 1980s for cars as diverse as the Marina and the Metro, yet in the early 1960s that engine size did not yet exist. The engine developed for the Mini-Cooper S, in fact, was eventually 'productionised' for use by the masses.

Compared with earlier A-series engines including the 997cc Mini-Cooper unit, two major changes, in construction and layout, had to be made. One was that the cylinder bore centres in the block casting were juggled around so that a larger bore could be used and the other was that the head casting was revised, not only to give better breathing but to incorporate an extra holding-down stud.

The first derivative, which was produced in a real hurry, was the 1,071cc unit, which used the new 'S' bore of 70.64mm but retained the 68.26mm stroke of the 850 Mini. The reasons were all connected with what production machinery could be altered with the least disruption to other A-series assembly and at the lowest investment cost. In fact, not only was it convenient to machine the new S-type's EN40B steel crankshaft on existing tooling but it helped produce a high-revving oversquare power unit. Even so, it was only intended as an interim power unit while the two definitive 'S' engines were finalised.

The 1,275cc version of the 'S' engine came next, using the same sturdy new cylinder block but using a new long-stroke crankshaft and 81.33mm stroke. This, in fact, was the same stroke as that used in the 997cc Mini-Cooper engine (which, translated into good old Imperial measure, was 3.2in exactly!).

Finally (deliveries of cars with this engine did not begin until June 1964) came the 970cc 'S' engine, still with the same block and large bore but with a unique 61.91mm stroke, which was never used in any other A-series engine: by any standards, this was an 'homologation special' power unit, solely produced to get sporting approval for the ultimate in 1-litre Mini-Coopers...

Left: This restored Mini-Cooper S engine/transmission unit shows just how compact the twin-SU version of the front-wheel-drive package actually was.

Still usable by the district nurse

When Ford was developing the Escort Twin Cam, and later the RS1600, it made few compromises over engine design, as scope for tuning was considered much more important than flexibility. BMC, on the other hand, was not as ruthless. Years later, Competitions Manager Stuart Turner commented that the Mini-Cooper S would have been a much better sports saloon '...if Sales hadn't insisted that it be usable by the district nurse!'.

How many district nurses used Mini-Cooper S models when they were on the market? Not many, I'm sure, but BMC and its dealers had generations of history to live up to – which meant that the 'S' had to be easy to drive and flexible in heavy traffic.

Although the 'S' engines were a lot more powerful than those of ordinary Minis – the 1275S, after all, had 76bhp, which was 224 per cent more than the 850 Mini – they could have been a whole lot more torquey, especially if a more sporty camshaft grind had been specified. But you, of course, know all that, don't you? An entire tuning industry grew up to rectify BMC's blinkered 'district nurse' mentality.

Even the 970S (a high-revving, limited-production car) was still a totally practical road car, with the same equipment, sound deadening, instruments, and seating as other Mini-Coopers – yet it was this car, more than any other Mini, which BMC needed to dominate the 1.0-litre class in racing and rallying. Since only 1,000 such cars had to be sold, the company would put little marketing effort behind that model...

Left: Sixteen-bladed cooling fans were fitted from late 1961, in an effort to reduce engine noise while maintaining cooling efficiency.

Mini-Cooper S on sale: an eight-year life

Although the 1275S dominates the sales statistics – 33,824 of the 38,818 'S' saloons built used the 1,275cc engine – it shared BMC sales with the other types until April 1965.

The original model was the 1071S, introduced in March 1963, which shared the same different-colour roof livery with Mini-Coopers, its only external identification being the 'S' badges on the bonnet and boot lids, and the new pierced wheels. As ever, there was rubber-cone suspension, while Austin and Morris-badged versions, with different grilles, were sold through different dealer chains.

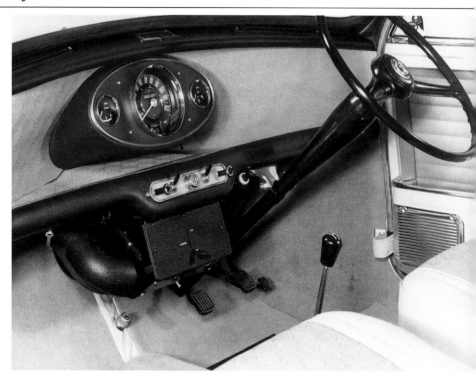

Right: Externally, the only visual differences between Mini-Cooper and Mini-Cooper S types were the 'S' badges at front and rear.

Left: By 1964 there were no fewer than three different types of Mini-Cooper S on sale – with 970cc, 1,071cc, and 1,275cc engines – but only the 1,275cc version was the big survivor.

From this angle – pure side view – it is impossible to pick out a Cooper S from a less special Mini of the mid-1960s, though the wheel and the front bumper details give the game away.

The good news for those ready to pay £695 (yes, peanuts by today's standards but we thought that was quite expensive in those days) was that 145-10in radial-ply tyres, servo-assisted brakes, and a fresh-air heater were all standard.

However, that was really a short-run model. Though Paddy Hopkirk's legendary Monte Carlo Rally win of 1964 came in a 1071S, BMC never planned to keep it on after the 1275S was available. Soon after the 1275S went on sale in the spring of 1964, production of the 1071S was wound down and the last of all was produced in August 1964. This means that all the genuine production cars had 'dry' suspension.

The 970S and 1275S models were introduced in April 1964 – according to the publicity announcements, at least,

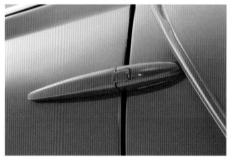

Left: Way back in the late 1950s, the Mini's designers saved money by providing external door hinges. These would remain until the ADO 20 facelift, which followed in 1969.

Far left: As on all early-type Minis, the Mini-Cooper S of the 1960s used simple plastic catches on the door windows.

Left: Alec Issigonis's original vision was to have sliding windows on every version of the Mini. Until the felt running channels became sodden with rainwater, when the glass tended to stick, this was a very practical alternative to a wind-up mechanism.

Although it was only 10ft long, the Mini-Cooper S of the 1960s offered a formidably capable performance package. All such cars carried the 'S' badge on the nose, it being quite impossible to know which of three engines was actually fitted. This is a 970S.

Below: On this car, a mid-1960s Mini-Cooper S, the turn indicators are standard: many owners had these replaced by larger, back-fixing, driving lamps.

Below right: Simple, informative – and proud. Who needs a stylist?

for the truth is that the 970S was not yet ready to go on sale. Stuart Turner remembers that just one road car was available when he applied for homologation in mid-1964, that some BMC top manager wrote a letter confirming that 1,000 cars had been produced – and that sporting homologation was achieved on that basis: 'We had one car. Just one car. We sent it everywhere for the first few months – dealer showrooms, displays, racing circuits – just so that the RAC was convinced that we had made all the cars!'

Above: Although all Cooper S models were assembled at Longbridge, some were Austins and others were Morris types. Technically, there was absolutely no difference between the brands.

Above middle: Even by the mid-1960s, the boot area of Mini-Coopers and Mini-Cooper Ss was still very simply trimmed. With the fuel tank to one side, and a rigid floor above the spare wheel and the battery, there was precious little space for stowage.

Above: The extra tubular quarter bumper/overriders fitted to this Mini-Cooper 970S were decorative but really had no safety function.

Left: Everyone being passed by such a car only needed to look at the badge on the boot lid – Austin Cooper S – to realise why...

55

Right: When fitted with sliding windows (between 1961 and 1969) all Mini-Cooper and Cooper S types had these amazingly capacious storage bins inside the doors.

Right: Early-type Minis, including this 1965 Cooper S, had external swivel-type door handles. There was one famous occasion when a 'works' rally car left a timing point with the marshal's watch and sling trapped inside the open end!

Right: In the 1960s, everyone loved the Cooper S for its combination of character, performance, compact dimensions, and sheer youthful appeal.

Above: Like all mid-1960s Cooper S types, the engine bay of this 970S is well filled. Externally it is impossibly to 'pick' a 970S from a 1275S, for all cars had the same external manifolding, twin SU carburettors, and air trunking for the fresh air heater.

This wide-angle camera shot flatters the space in the driving compartment of the Mini-Cooper S. Although such cars (and Mini-Coopers, of course) had effective little remote-control gear changes, they still had the same two-spoke steering wheels and the very vertical column alignment of all other Minis.

BMC, in fact, was honest after the event, for 1,000 engines were eventually made. In fact, BMC dealers rarely stocked the 970S, which cost £693, making it a special-order model and eventually delivered 963 cars before officially dropping the model in April 1965. In round figures, half the run had 'dry' suspension, the second half having Hydrolastic, which was phased in from September 1964.

Left: Drivers wanting to enjoy the performance of the Mini-Cooper S had to make do with the same upright seating position as all other Minis and the tiny pedals, which had to live inboard of the front wheel-boxes.

Left: In the mid-1960s, Mini-Cooper S drivers had the luxury of scanning a three-dial instrument panel. The speedometer read up to 120mph, which was a very generous provision, for no Cooper S could even reach 100mph.

Cooper and Cooper S in motor sport

Two important events changed the motor sport scene at Abingdon in the autumn of 1961. One was that the original Mini-Cooper was announced, the other being the arrival of a new, young, and ambitious Competitions Manager, Stuart Turner. Not only was the Cooper eminently suitable for use in races and rallies but Turner was ruthlessly ambitious and determined to make it so.

Telling this part of the story is made easy because Turner almost immediately decided on a two-prong strategy – that Abingdon would concentrate entirely on rallying (which, as a successful co-driver, was Turner's first love), while works-assisted motor racing would be contracted out, originally to the Cooper Car Co and later to Ken Tyrrell as well.

'Works' rally cars

Starting in 1962, the 997cc Mini-Cooper immediately became a winner. Though Rauno Aaltonen's entry in the Monte Carlo Rally ended in a fiery crash, that formidable young lady Pat Moss fell in love with 737 ABL, not only winning the Tulip and German rallies but also winning the European Ladies' Championship too. By the end of the year, Turner had decided to build up a new fleet of Mini-Coopers and the strategy worked well.

Rauno Aaltonen placed fifth on the 1962 RAC Rally, then took a magnificent third in the 1963 Monte, with Paddy Hopkirk sixth. Paddy then took second overall in the Tulip (only a 4.2-litre Ford Falcon could outpace him) but it was in the hot, often high and always demanding French Alpine where Rauno got his hands on the very first 1,071cc-engined Mini-Cooper S and astonished the rallying world by winning the entire Touring category.

Three months later Paddy Hopkirk and Henry Liddon shared another brand-new 1071S (33 EJB) to finish third overall in the Touring Car category of the 10-day Tour de France. Almost from that day forward, Abingdon lost all interest in improving the 997cc car (and never even took a later 998cc car on to the strength).

It was a wise decision. Not only did Paddy finish fourth in the RAC Rally (in 1071S 8 EMO) but two months after that, in the never-to-be-forgotten Monte Carlo Rally of 1964, he won the event outright in 33 EJB. This was the first of a string of Cooper S outright victories, which would make the little car immortal.

Far left: Paddy Hopkirk, Henry Liddon, and their Mini-Cooper 1071S recorded a sensational victory in the 1964 Monte Carlo Rally...

Left: ...which meant that they were invited to appear on ITV's Sunday Night at the London Palladium TV show. Here they were entering the back door of the theatre.

Even so, the avalanche of Cooper S rally wins was only just beginning. Abingdon entered its first 1275S (AJB 66B) in the 1964 Tulip rally, where Timo Makinen gave it a memorable debut victory. Fourth overall for Rauno Aaltonen in the French Alpine rally and fourth for Timo in the 1000 Lakes added to the success of the 1275S in its first season – but the best was yet to come.

Right: Perhaps the most famous Mini rally victory of all? Paddy Hopkirk Mini-Cooper 1071S won the 1964 Monte Carlo Rally in 33 EJB, after a titanic struggle against Bo Ljungfeldt's 4.7-litre Ford Falcon.

Far right: Five proud men pose in front of Paddy Hopkirk's now-legendary 33 EJB Monte-winning Mini-Cooper 1071S. Left to right are: Bill Appleby (BMC Chief Engine Designer), Daniel Richmond (Downton), John Cooper, Charles Griffin, and Alec Issigonis.

Right: By the time BMC's 'works' mechanics had completed preparation of a Mini-Cooper S rally car, the engine bay was completely full. Extra cockpit heating was fitted to this car, which was being readied for the Monte Carlo Rally.

Early Mini rally victories

1962	Tulip (Pat Moss)	Mini-Cooper 997cc
1962	German (Pat Moss)	Mini-Cooper 997cc
1963	French Alpine (Rauno Aaltonen)	Cooper S 1,071cc
1964	Monte Carlo (Paddy Hopkirk)	Cooper S 1,071cc
1964	Tulip (Timo Makinen)	Cooper S 1,275cc

Works-supported racecars

No sooner had the 997cc Mini-Cooper been put on sale and gained FIA Homologation, than BMC hired the Cooper Car Co to campaign cars on its behalf in the BRSCC British Saloon Car Championship. Recognisable from the very start by their glossy green finish and the two broad wide fore-aft stripes painted on the extremes of the bonnet, these two cars (one driven by John Love, the other by Sir John Whitmore) dominated their 1-litre class, though Christabel Carlisle, driving a privately-financed car that had been prepared by Don Moore, astonished everyone else with her pace and flair.

In 1962, although a fleet of Jaguar 3.8-litre Mk2s were habitual race winners, John Love's 997cc 'Cooper Cooper' comfortably won his class enough times,

for no other 1-litre car could match the pace of this little front-wheel-drive car. Although it was not quite the same story again in 1963 (Ford had latched on to the 'homologation special' business, producing the Cortina-Lotus), John Whitmore used 997cc, then 1,071cc, Minis to win his capacity class on most occasions and to take second in the Championship: Paddy Hopkirk backed him up all the way.

Things got even more serious in 1964. In Britain, not only had Ford rolled out a mass of Cortina-Lotus (the F1 World Champion drove one) and Galaxie entries but BMC now had the formidable 100bhp-plus 1275S for the 1.3-litre class. Clark's

Cortina-Lotus was powerful enough to win several races outright but John Fitzpatrick's 1275S easily won the 1.3-litre category and took second in the Championship.

Meantime, BMC hired Ken Tyrrell's team to run two works-supported Mini-Cooper S types in the European Saloon Car Championship, once again with an eye to winning their class and taking best advantage of the favourable class marking position. Warwick Banks, John Rhodes, and the Belgian driver Julien Vernaeve all drove them. The result was that Warwick Banks easily won his class and the European Championship. The Mini racing phenomenon was really on a roll.

Upgrading the 850 Mini

In the autumn of 1961, although this was quite overshadowed by the launch of the Mini-Cooper, BMC also announced an enlargement to the standard-engined range of Minis. The new type, badged Super Seven/Super Mini-Minor, was really a halfway house towards the Mini-Cooper, for it had the same type of duotone colour scheme and the extra corner bumpers, along with slightly different front grilles. Like the Cooper, too, the Super inherited a rigid platform over the spare

wheel/battery locations in the boot, along with the three-dial instrument panel display and lever-type interior door handles. Priced at £591 17s 3d (£591.86), the Super cost only £24 more than the Mini De Luxe but was still £87 cheaper than the new Mini-Cooper.

More marketing, rather than technical, action then followed. Early in 1962, BMC finally fell in line with public opinion, dropping the 'Se7en' and 'Mini-Minor' names. Henceforth, all cars would merely be called 'Mini' – which,

Mini versus 1100: a comparison

When the Morris 1100 was launched in 1962, it shared the same basic engine, transmission, and suspension layout as that of the Mini but was widely different in many ways:

Feature	Mini	Morris 1100
Engine	848cc	1,098cc
Power	34bhp	48bhp
Front suspension	Rubber cone	Hydrolastic units
Body style	2-door saloon	4-door saloon
	3-door estate	
Length	10ft 0¼in	12ft 2¾in
Width	4ft 7in	5ft 0⅜in
Height	4ft 5in	4ft 4¾in
Unladen weight	1,380lb	1,820lb
Total price (Sept 1962)	£535 De Luxe	£695 4-door De Luxe

Above: Theme and variations – the Super de Luxe type of 850 was launched in 1962, still with the standard single-carburettor engine but with all the Mini-Cooper's trim and extra decoration. This one is badged as a Morris.

as far as the public was concerned, was what they had been all along – though there would still be separate Austin and Morris types for more than seven years to follow.

The next reshuffle took place in October 1962, when both the De Luxe and Super models were replaced by a single derivative to be known as Super de Luxe. Hidden away, as in the latest Mini-Coopers, was baulk-ring synchromesh in the gearbox, with cosmetic changes being restricted to the use of yet another new grille and better-quality Vynide upholstery. Fortuitously, immediately after the London Motor Show of October 1962, a reduction in British purchase tax meant that all Minis became cheaper.

For 1963, therefore, this was the line-up:

Mini (basic)	£447 12s 11d
Mini Super de Luxe	£492 19s 2d
Mini Traveller/ Countryman	£531 12s 6d
Mini-Cooper	£567 17s 6d

Although no further major changes would be made until the autumn of 1964, the Mini range was already beginning to look quite complex, for two rather different long-nose/long-tail derivatives – badged as Rileys or Wolseleys – had joined in.

Left: BMC rang the changes with Mini names and specifications in the early 1960s, this being the Austin Super de Luxe of 1963, as pictured from the front...

Below: ...and the rear.

Left: In the early days, one could buy a Basic or De Luxe, Austin or Morris model. The Super variety, with this type of grille and extra corner bumpers, followed on in 1961. This was the Austin version...

Riley Elf and Wolseley Hornet variants

Two new Mini-derived types, the Riley Elf and the Wolseley Hornet arrived in October 1961. These cars shared the same bodyshell and the same running gear. So why two new models and not one? Why 'badge engineered'? Why so obviously the same products but with slightly different party frocks?

One had to be there to understand this – for at the time BMC still controlled separate dealer franchises, which still competed fiercely with each other. Although Riley and Wolseley had both been in the same (Nuffield Organisation) group since 1938, after more than 20 years neither marque had died away – and neither seemed to have suffered.

Looked at today, this might seem crazy but there is no doubt that BMC's 'badge engineering' policy succeeded, for sales certainly increased. As not many imported cars were coming to the UK at this time, BMC's 'different badge in every showroom' policy certainly gave British drivers something to think about when they were planning their next purchase!

Both cars revived famous 1930s sports-car model names. The small Riley was badged Elf, after a two-seater model of 1935, whereas the Wolseley Hornet was named after that company's early-1930s six-cylinder offerings.

Although these cars were obviously based on the existing Mini 'platform' wheelbase, front-wheel-drive installation, and rubber-cone independent suspensions, their two-door bodyshells were considerably different, both at the front and at the rear. Because they had longer tails, the cars' overall length had gone up by 8½in.

Although the front wings and general structure were much the same, there was no sign of the Mini's outward-turned panel joints at first and there was a new front style, where much of the usual Austin/Morris grille area had been filled in by an inner transverse panel and traditional-style grilles were fixed to new-shape bonnet pressings (which meant that when the bonnets were raised, the grilles came up and forward, too). These, in fact, were the first Minis to have lockable bonnets. In both cases, there were additional supplementary side grilles and unique side/indicator lamps.

At the rear, the floorpan was lengthened behind the line of the rear wheels. Rear wings were elongated by several inches, almost like mini-fins, with new-style stop/tail/indicator lamp clusters, these surrounding a new upward-opening boot lid 'bustle'. The result was an 8cu ft boot, compared with the 5.5cu ft in the original Minis.

BMC planners had been able to give these cars the same air of luxury as was suggested in the marques' larger models. Both cars had a wider colour range than the Austin/Morris types, with roof panels always painted in a contrasting colour, bigger and plusher two-tone seating,

(Rileys with cloth facings, Wolseleys with cloth-simulating plastic), and a rigid (carpeted) cover over the spare wheel and battery in the boot.

BMC's product planners also decided to give the new Riley a slightly more upper-bracket package than the Wolseley – and BMC was able to charge more money for it. Accordingly, the Elf cost £693 18s 11d (£693.94) at launch, the Hornet £672 1s 5d (£672.07) – a £22 difference, which is equivalent to perhaps £300 at today's values.

Whereas the Wolseley had the traditional illuminated Wolseley grille badge at the front and a Mini-Cooper type of instrument panel with three dials (but with wood veneer facing), the Elf deployed those same three dials in a unique manner in a centrally positioned slab of burr walnut and had a chrome-plated gear lever.

Interestingly enough, the Elf first shown in October 1961 had open parcels shelves at each side of the instrument panel but by the time deliveries began this arrangement had been changed, to incorporate full-width wood panels and twin drop-down glove lockers. Fitting a radio meant hanging it under the parcels shelf on the passenger's side.

BMC, however, never left its detail specifications alone for very long. Visible front wing panel joints (original Mini-style) were reintroduced – they had been absent on prototype and launch cars

– along with front and rear bumper overriders in the spring of 1962, closely followed by the improved baulk-ring type of synchromesh being fitted to all Minis of the period.

Above left: Before and after! Original-type Riley Elf/Wolseley Hornets had hidden welded panel joints on the front wing but...

Above: ...these re-appeared again within a year of production starting up.

Left: One way of making the Riley Elf different from the Wolseley Hornet was to provide this wall-to-wall wooden facia with separate gloveboxes and a unique instrument arrangement, though the long direct-action gear lever remained. The Hornet, on the other hand, had a Mini-Cooper oval instrument cluster (though with a wooden facing) and remote-control gear change.

Elf and Hornet MkII developments

Because these cars evolved in their own unique way, I have grouped some of that change into this chapter, even though the story overlaps into the next two chapters.

From March 1963, MkII models took over. Theses featured a new 998cc derivative of the A-series engine and, although the peak power and torque improvements were not startling, the new engine was altogether more flexible and torquey at all points.

Spotters found it difficult to pick out the new models. Except for the fitment of 'MkII' badges on the boot lid, there were no visual style changes, and virtually none to the cabin, though the lift-up boot lid now had counter-balancing springs and the front brakes had 1½in wide instead of 1¼in wide shoes with a twin leading-shoe arrangement.

Because of a recent UK purchase tax reduction (which came into effect in November 1962), the MkII Elf and Hornet prices were actually lower than they had been in 1961 – £574 10s 5d (£574.52) and £556 8s 0d (£556.40) respectively, the Riley still being slightly more expensive.

The 998cc-engined car was certainly faster than the original 848cc machine and it was definitely easier to keep it moving comfortably at a 65–70mph cruising pace. Unless one was absolutely flat out, it was quite easy to get close to 40mpg on long runs.

The specification then settled down to a period of stability, though from late 1964 the Elf/Hornet cars picked up the same mechanical innovations as ordinary Minis – Hydrolastic suspension, diaphragm spring clutch, and a facia-mounted starter/ignition switch: these will be more fully described in the next chapter.

Hydrolastic suspension still relied on rubber cone springs but these were backed by a water-based liquid under high pressure, the front units being connected to the rear units by slim pipes. If the chassis had time to react when a front wheel went over a bump, this gave a degree of self-levelling to the car, for the rear suspension dropped, to suit. In fact, the Hydrolastic suspension gave a softer, rather more floaty, ride than the original rubber system and was retained until the end of Elf/Hornet production.

Above: From 1963, the Elf/Hornet twins became MkII, with single-carburettor 998cc engines.

Right: Film Star Peter Sellers ordered this Mini-Cooper S in 1963 and had it customised, complete with fake (painted) canework.

Mini production

In the meantime, the rest of the Mini range had become more complex, more various, and more appealing, with production rising steadily. Some 216,087 Minis of all types had been produced in 1962 but two years later production had risen even further – to 244,359. With the millionth Mini about to roll off the track at Longbridge, and with much more technical novelty planned, the next few years would be very adventurous.

Mini production in the market-place

Calendar year	Mini (all models)	BMC (all models)*	Total UK car production
1959	19,749	431,247	1,189,943
1960	116,677	585,096	1,352,728
1961	157,059	510,318	1,003,967
1962	216,087	525,793	1,249,426
1963	236,713	637,803	1,607,939
1964	244,359	730,862	1,867,640

* The only figures available cover the BMC financial year, 1 August to 31 July inclusive

Specifications: Riley Elf and Wolseley Hornet MkI and MkII

ENGINE

Description
In-line four-cylinder with cast iron block and cylinder head. Chain-driven camshaft in block, pushrod-operated overhead valves. Heart-shaped combustion chambers. Aluminium alloy pistons, forged steel connecting rods. Three-bearing counter-weighted crankshaft

Capacity
MkI 848cc (51.8cu in)
MkII 998cc (60.9cu in)

Bore and stroke
MkI 62.94mm x 68.26mm (2.48in x 2.68in)
MkII 64.59mm x 76.2mm (2.54in x 3.00in)

Compression ratio
8.3:1

Maximum power
MkI 34bhp @ 5,500rpm
MkII 38bhp @ 5,250rpm

Maximum torque
MkI 44lb ft (59Nm) @ 2,900rpm
MkII 52lb ft (70Nm) @ 2,700rpm

Carburettor
Single 1¼in SU HS2

TRANSMISSION

Gearbox
Four-speed with synchromesh on top three gears (all synchromesh from summer 1968). Optional Automotive Products four-speed automatic from late 1967

Ratios	Manual	Automatic
1st	3.627:1	2.690:1
2nd	2.171:1	1.851:1
3rd	1.414:1	1.458:1
Top	1.000:1	1.000:1
Reverse	3.627:1	2.690:1

Clutch
Borg and Beck, 7⅛in Single dry plate (diaphragm spring from late 1964)

Final drive
Helical spur gears, ratio: 3.765:1

BRAKES

Front
Lockheed drum, 7in x 1½in

Rear
Lockheed drum, 7in x 1½in

Operation
Lockheed hydraulic

Handbrake
Lever, with cable linkage to rear drums

SUSPENSION

Front
Independent, rubber cone springs (Hydrolastic suspension units, with hydraulic connection to rear suspension, from late 1964), double wishbones, telescopic dampers

Rear
Independent, rubber cone springs (Hydrolastic suspension units, with hydraulic connection to front suspension, from late 1964), trailing arms, telescopic dampers

STEERING

Type
Rack and pinion

Number of turns lock to lock
2¾

Turning circle
32ft 0in (9.75m) approx, between kerbs

Steering wheel
Two spoke, 15.75in diameter

WHEELS AND TYRES
3½J x 10in steel disc wheels

Tyres
5.20-10in cross-ply

PERFORMANCE
The Autocar road tests:
Riley Elf MkI 2 March 1962
Wolseley Hornet MkII 16 August 1963

Top speed
Riley Elf MkI 71mph (114kph)
Wolseley Hornet MkII 77mph (123kph)

Acceleration
0–30mph (48kph)	6.9sec	6.0sec
0–50mph (80kph)	18.3sec	15.7sec
0–60mph (96kph)	32.3sec	24.1sec
Standing quarter mile (402m)	23.7sec	22.4sec

Overall fuel consumption
Riley Elf MkI 32.9mpg (8.6l/100km)
Wolseley Hornet MkII 35.3mpg (8.0l/100km)

DIMENSIONS

Length
10ft 8¾in (3,272mm)

Width
4ft 7in (1,397mm)

Height
4ft 5in (1,346mm)

Wheelbase
6ft 8½in (2,036mm)

Track
Front: 3ft 11⅜in (1,205mm)
Rear: 3ft 9⅞in (1,165mm)

Ground Clearance
7⅛in (181mm)

Unladen weight
1,393lb (632kg)

1964–1967
Mokes, Hydrolastic Minis, and automatic transmission

Five years on from the original launch of the Mini, 1964 was a big year for the brand. Not only did we see the arrival of the Mini-Cooper 1275S (already described) but it was also the year in which the quirky Mini-Moke made its bow and in which Hydrolastic suspension took over from rubber cone springs on all the saloons. More than that, although the general public was not let in on the secret at the time, an automatic transmission option was also on the way.

Before giving a year-on-year analysis of which Minis used what feature, and when, first of all those two features are described in detail.

Hydrolastic: liquid innovation

Hydrolastic suspension – the use of a water/alcohol-based fluid to link rubber-cone suspension, front-to-rear – had been invented by Dr Alex Moulton of Moulton Developments in the 1950s. Moulton, who became a great friend of Alec Issigonis, had urged that this system should be fitted to original Minis but it was not yet fully developed and was significantly more costly than the simple rubber cone suspension that took its place.

However, development work continued and the original layout was adopted on the front-wheel-drive Austin/Morris 1100 model, which was introduced in August 1962. Because this was a great success with

Left: The changeover fr[...] 'dry' (rubber cone) to '[...] (Hydrolastic) suspensio[...] took place in the autu[...] of 1964. This shows jus[...] how compact the entir[...] engine/transmission/ front suspension/steeri[...] subframe assembly actually was. The Hydrolastic giveaway is the tubes sprouting from the top of the suspension units.

he clientele, and the dealer chain rapidly got used to it, development work on Minis continued, such that it was introduced in October 1964. It was the joint genius of Issigonis, Moulton, and their respective design teams that made it possible for Hydrolastic suspension units to fit within unaltered Mini subframes and for the pipework linking front to rear suspension to be neatly aligned under the floorpan along the central 'services' tunnel.

As perfected for production, Hydrolastic suspension was an excellent example of co-operation. The principal inspiration had come from Moulton Developments, of Bradford-on-Avon in Wiltshire, packaging and finalisation was by BMC at Longbridge, and mass production was carried out by the Dunlop Rubber Co in the Midlands.

Each sealed Hydrolastic unit was of a similar size and bulk to the original rubber spring, which it replaced. Inside it there was rubber as the main suspension medium, some carefully controlled valves to allow a liquid to pass through (these valves acting as dampers), with front and rear suspension units on the same side of the car interconnected by liquid-filled small-diameter tubes. There was no pitch-damping, this being ensured by careful calibration of the pipework and the fittings around the units.

It was because of the use of liquid that Hydrolastic soon became known as 'wet' suspension – as opposed to 'dry' where rubber cone springs were concerned. The fluid itself, incidentally, was 49 per cent water, 49 per cent methyl alcohol (as used in anti-freeze), with a dash of rust inhibitor and a distasteful dye intended to make the mixture unpalatable.

That liquid, incidentally, was installed at very high pressure and, because of the inevitable leakages over time, BMC dealers were equipped to 'pump up' the systems before they sagged too much. Because separate telescopic suspension dampers were no longer needed, those previously used on 'dry' Minis were discarded. There was no supplementary control at the front but at the rear, in place of the damper, there was a narrow diameter sheathed tension spring to tune the behaviour of the car.

Not only did this system give a softer (albeit rather bouncier) ride than the original rubber cone layout but on undulating roads and tracks it also gave a modicum of self-levelling. Unless speeds were very high, when the front wheels of a Hydrolastic-equipped car went over sizeable bumps, there was just time for liquid transfer through the pipes to jack up the rear suspension in time to compensate.

Hydrolastic was not, on the other hand, devoid of limitations. When the Mini was heavily laden, up to the limits of its payload capacity, it tended to drive along with its tail relatively further down than the old rubber-suspended models had ever done. Those with sensitive stomachs sometimes complained that the ride could make them feel queasy (for a dealer to 'pump up' the liquid pressure was not a valid cure), also every BMC dealer had to learn all about the quirks of the installation and to install hydraulic pumping machinery to keep the ride height of the car up to spec.

This facility, though, should not be over-emphasised; a downside was that there was also a tendency to set up something of rocking-horse motion. Where motor sport was concerned, exhaustive back-to-back testing showed that it seemed to suit some drivers but not others so, where company

politics (and regulations!) required it, Hydrolastic was fitted to the cars but sometimes craftily rendered inoperable through hidden cut-off taps under the rear seats!

Nevertheless, BMC policy was to introduce Hydrolastic suspension, instead of rubber cone suspension, for every Mini saloon – 850, Mini-Cooper, Cooper S, Elf, and Hornet – from the start of building 1965 Model Year cars. However, it was not fitted at all to the load-carrying estate cars, vans, pick-ups, or Mokes. As it transpired, the use of Hydrolastic suspension would always be controversial, not only the grounds of its behaviour (see the previous comment regarding queasy passengers) but because the dealers were not happy with the extra technology they had to use to maintain it (it would also be standardised on BMC 1100, 1800, and Maxi models, of course), and because of its cost.

After the balance of engineering power had changed following the formation of British Leyland, Hydrolastic was put under sentence of death: because of this, most mainstream Minis would revert to 'dry' suspension after 1969 and it was never used under the new long-nose Clubman/1275GT types at all.

Above: When the Mini's suspension was converted from 'dry' (rubber cones) to 'wet' (Hydrolastic) in 1964, the Hydrolastic units fitted remarkably easily into the little car's structure.

Automatic transmission

Almost as soon as the original Mini went on sale, Automotive Products of Leamington Spa started work on a technically exciting little automatic transmission system for use in this front-wheel-drive car. Although AP had never before tackled such a major programme, few doubted its technical ability to do a great job, as two of its other activities were to manufacture Lockheed disc and drum brakes, and Borg & Beck clutches.

Designing, fitting, and finalising automatic transmission for the Mini was ambitious, groundbreaking, stuff, for no one else in the world had yet tackled such a thing. Although DAF's 590cc front-engined Daffodil (by 1964 enlarged to 746cc) had been sold with its Variomatic belt-driven rear-mounted automatic transmission since 1958, all other automatic transmission cars used at least 1.5-litre engines: no one, but no one, had put an automatic-transmission front-wheel-drive car on the market.

Working on the basis that no one had told it this could not be done, AP set out to break the mould, not only by placing a four-speed automatic transmission in the sump of a Mini (it took the place of the existing manual transmission) but arranging for it to share the same lubricant as that of the engine, something that transmission engineers did not like but which seemed to work out well in practice. In fact, the new AP box was the very first British-engineered system to go into production.

This was done remarkably neatly: the engine/transmission installation was carried out tidily, no one really noticed the absence of a clutch pedal, the gear selector lever was placed unobtrusively in the centre of the floor ahead of/between the seats, and the only external evidence was an 'Automatic' badge on the boot lid.

Those were the days in which power loss through the torque converter, and its effect on fuel economy, was a big factor. BMC therefore set AP a particularly arduous task, not only in reducing such losses but in packaging the installation so that it would fit in/under/around the existing Mini engine and engine bay. This was done by installing the torque converter where the manual clutch would normally go and by placing the complex epicyclic gears under the engine crankshaft, exactly as the normal manual gears were located.

This is not the place to describe the internal workings of a four-speed automatic (let's not even go there...): it is enough to point out that the automatic box used the same spur-gear final drive ratio as the manual car (3.765:1) and that power losses through the torque converter were remarkably small.

For the Mini, AP's true innovation was in what choice was provided in the selector quadrant, which was placed on the floor of the car (in those days, most automatics had column-mounted levers), with straightforward fore-and-aft actuation. Instead of having a conventional PRNDL (Park-Reverse-Neutral-Drive-Low), the Mini offered RN1234D.

Normally, therefore, the driver would select D (for Drive) and let automatic controls do the rest, with the usual kick-down feature available only from top (fourth) ratio to third. Even so, by using '3' '2', and '1' it was effectively possible to use the new installation as a manual transmission with clutch-less change. An important extra feature was the use of a freewheel which operated only on the first ratio. If '1' was selected when the car was moving too fast, it would not engage and a a consequence no engine braking was provided on the overrun.

In getting this major option accepted, BMC had two problems. The first was an habitual problem at this time – that the launch (in October 1965) came many

Below: Laurence Watts's remarkable cutaway drawing, as published in Autocar *in 1965, shows all the complexities of the four-speed automatic transmission, which AP developed for the Mini (and later, for 1100/1300 models too).*

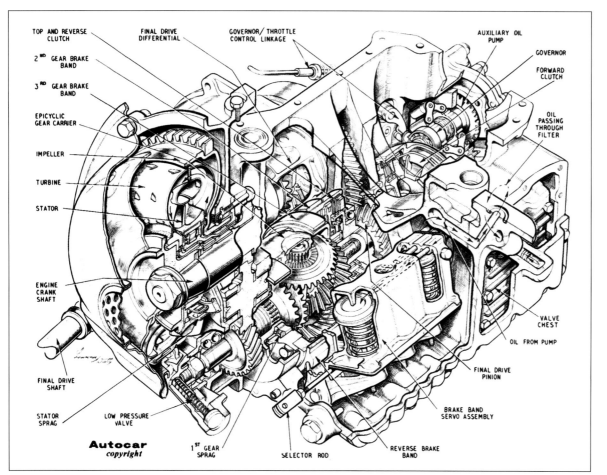

months before deliveries could actually take place – but the other was in justifying the price asked for the car. In 1965, for instance, a manual-transmission Mini Super de Luxe cost £515 2s 1d (£515.10) in the UK, while automatic transmission bumped that up by another £90 12s 6d (£90.62).

Because cost inflation has made such a mockery of prices in the four decades since then, perhaps £90 does not sound much – but it added 17.5 per cent to the price. Put in modern terms, that would mean asking a latter-day MINI owner to pay up to £2,000 for the pleasure of a clutch-less change (which is almost double that actually asked).

Originally available only on 848cc-engined Minis, the AP automatic would eventually be adopted for other and larger-engined Minis (as we shall see), for most of the larger 1100/1300 family, and would continue to be an extra-cost option on the Mini (but never on Mini-Coopers) until 1996.

How the automatic Mini performed

When *Autocar* tested an automatic (Austin) Mini in October 1965, the writer conducted that test and wrote the report. Compared with a normal manual Mini, it was instructive to see that although the actual performance of the car was little affected, the fuel consumption was about ten per cent worse than before, as this table confirms:

	Automatic (1965 test)	Manual (1963 test)
Top speed	70.5mph	71.8mph
0–60mph	32.0sec	29.7sec
Standing quarter mile (402m)	24.3sec	23.6sec
Overall fuel consumption	33.1mpg	36.6mpg

When I re-read my own words, I see that my summary concluded: 'Older people will appreciate the reduced effort and concentration demanded...the versatility of his new transmission, so adaptable to traffic conditions or to one's mood, is bound to "sell" it also to many keen drivers who would not tolerate being confined to automatic gear-changing for all their motoring.'

Changes for 1965 – and a new Mini Moke

From September 1964, and quite apart from the standardisation of Hydrolastic suspension for all the saloons, all non-Coopers gained two-leading-shoe front drum brakes and diaphragm spring clutches, while the use of a key starter for the engine (instead of the button on the floor) was standardised for all types. Non-Coopers inherited stronger gearboxes to match those fitted to Coopers and the Elf/Hornet derivatives all followed suit.

In the meantime, yet another version of this now famous car had now appeared – the Mini Moke. Yes, of course, every Mini enthusiast remembers that brightly decorated Mini Mokes were used in that enigmatic 1960s TV series *The Prisoner* but not all of them remember that the car was originally designed with a much more serious purpose. If BMC had had its way, the British Army would have bought Mokes in large numbers!

It was an odd project, in a way, for the Army was only really interested if the Moke could be used as an off-tarmac-road vehicle and keep going in very rugged conditions. Now, you and I know that a Mini is one of the most agile vehicles in the world but a combination of 10in wheels and the need to carry four sturdy soldiers over rough ground was always going to be difficult.

This explains why the very first prototype Moke ran in 1959, the first public sighting came in 1960, a major redesign and a name change followed in 1962/1963, yet the car did not actually go on sale until August 1964. By that time, it was structurally unique, for although the Mini's front-wheel-drive power pack was carried over, together with the front and rear subframes and rubber-cone suspensions, the monocoque (or, more accurately, the platform-style chassis) was completely different.

Above left: When AP automatic transmission (optional from the winter of 1965/1966) was fitted to the Mini, the selector lever with its quadrant was placed in the centre of the floor, between the seats.

Above: Modifiers and customisers just loved to get their hands on the Mini – this being the Taurus company's offering on an 850, complete with its own brand of wooden dashboard, a rev counter in a pod on the steering column, and a gear-lever extension.

Left: London-based Harold Radford (Coachbuilders) Ltd, which had already made its name with special Countryman conversions on Rolls-Royce and Bentley models, also turned its hand to the Mini, producing the Mini de Ville in the mid-1960s.

Cheeky just standing there. Could the Mini-Moke possibly have more character than the original Mini? It certainly seemed like it.

Below: The engine/transmission/cooling installation of the Moke was exactly the same as that of other 848cc-engined Minis.

Moke design: like the Mini but different..

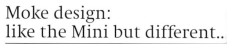

According to Laurence Pomeroy, who spent much time writing a BMC-sponsored book about the Mini (*The Mini Story*), in which Alec Issigonis was much involved: 'Early in the life of the Mini it was thought that a light personnel carrier could be evolved which would readily be airborne, would carry four men with light arms (or demolition gear), would sustain at least 60mph, and be so small that man-handling would be possible if it became stuck in cross-country work.'

This was a great idea but it was a notion that didn't really work at first. The first cars, nicknamed Buckboard, had unique pressed-steel platform hulls and were built on the standard Mini wheelbase. Revised cars with more ground clearance and a shortened wheelbase followed but once the world's military forces had lost interest, the Moke then had to be re-engineered for civilian sale.

Right: Although the rear suspension and structural subframe of the Moke were similar to those of the saloons, there were special details, enough to make parts provisioning a nightmare.

Right: Worm's eye view of the Mini Moke's 'dry' front suspension, almost exactly like that of the saloons, except for the all-weather tyre treads. Hydrolastic suspension would never be available on this model.

To keep Moke production as simple as possible (but nothing was simple, at BMC, in those days!), the final design had a unique hull but used almost all the 850 Mini's standard components, including the 34bhp/848cc engine, transmission, front and rear subframes, front and rear suspension, steering, and brakes.

The structure – hull, platform, chassis, how should this really be described? – was unique. Although it retained the standard Mini wheelbase, this was only for convenience, to make it easy to assemble on the production line. In fact, although parts of the Mini saloon's bulkhead and front toeboard pressings were retained, almost everything else was new. It was, in

Left: No special tooling here for the Moke's rear-end stop, tail, and indicator lamps, which all came out of Lucas's standard-parts bin.

Below: On a Mini Moke, one hoped that the battery would not need frequent attention, as it was tucked away inside one of the sills and accessed by two removable covers. Inconvenient but where else could it go?

Above: Having even a minor accident in a Mini Moke was not recommended, as the tubular front 'bumper' bent quite easily and the headlamps looked extremely vulnerable. Simple to repair, though – who needs a body shop?

This overhead shot confirms that the hull/tub/chassis/monocoque of the Mini Moke had very little in common with that of the Mini saloon and certainly did not share the same platform. No one, surely, ever bought a Moke as a shopping car, or runabout – where, for instance, would one stow the shopping bags or the valuables?

Above: This canvas 'tilt', with rather fragile-looking support poles, was standard equipment on the Moke but if an owner wanted sidescreens, he had to pay extra for them.

Below: Although the Mini Moke was a full four-seater, every passenger was completely exposed to the elements. Travelling in a Moke, in wet or cold weather, was not for the faint-hearted.

Moke on sale

When announced in August 1964 – naturally, for BMC at this time, with a choice of Austin or Morris badges – the Moke was priced at £335 (basic), or £406 7s 1d (£406.35) with purchase tax. That, of course, made the Moke significantly cheaper than the entry-level Mini 850 saloon, which was priced at £448 and would soon cost £470 when Hydrolastic suspension was adopted. When launched there was only one available colour – Spruce Green – a dark shade, which always tended to relate the Moke to BMC's commercial vehicles.

Cheaper, maybe, and with just about the same performance as a Mini 850 saloon, there were obvious drawbacks. Apart from the open-air motoring which came as standard (and bad-weather protection which was cheap and cheerful), for that money you only got one seat – for the driver.

To get a front passenger seat and a bench rear seat, you had to pay more, while other useful extras for off-road users were coarse-tread Dunlop Weathermaster tyres and a sump guard (which protected the engine/transmission casing from damage on rough roads but reduced the limited ground clearance even further). You could also order a heater but for an open car like this there didn't seem to be much point: it must have been about as effective as a candle in a hurricane.

fact, the first major departure from the Mini structural theme that had been revealed in 1959.

The structure, in fact, was a classic pressed-steel platform with torsion boxes along each flank, well boxed across the front and rear bulkheads but, of course, with no stiffening above waist level and no doors. There was a bumper bar – literally, a bar – at front and rear but no lockable luggage boot and no luxury.

Neither was that chassis platform as solid as it appeared at first, because

there were opening panels in the sills which reduced their torsional strength – these hid cubby boxes for stowage and, on one side, they also gave access to the battery. The petrol tank was also in the left-side sponson.

Independent suspension, by the way, was always by rubber cones: even after the rest of the Mini range converted to Hydrolastic at the end of 1964, the Moke kept its rubber.

Above: One big advantage of the Mini Moke's minimalist layout was that elbow-room was almost infinite. But it helped to be well-insulated and young at heart...

Below: The two-spoke steering wheel was the same as that fitted to the saloons but the instrument panel display was simple in the extreme. But then no one bought a Mini Moke for its luxury.

Until the customisers got their hands on one, every Mini Moke looked like this – four-square, stark, open to the elements, and painted in Spruce Green. There was only one wiper as standard, the second motor being an optional extra. British-built Mokes had 10in wheels – but these would be larger on Australian- and Portuguese-built examples.

Weather protection? Well, let's just say that in the British climate it helped to have a sense of humour. In high summer it was possible to fold the windscreen flat (or even take it off...) to enjoy the breeze but if it rained there was only a single wiper blade and the hood was a simple fold-up-and-over fabric 'tilt'. Although it was possible to buy voluminous floppy side curtains, which looked like afterthoughts (and were!), these were neither all-round water- nor wind-proof.

Inside the Moke, too, there were no carpets, no parcels shelf, and none of those invaluable door bins (there were no doors...), and since these were the days before safety belts were fitted, passengers had to use grab handles mounted on the sponsons to help hold themselves down!

Above: No passenger doors on a Mini Moke, of course, so access to the seats was made by climbing over the big, hollow, box-section sills. Depending on the

weather, some owners discarded the fold-back 'tilt' support irons but most people were grateful for the grab handles, which were provided on the sills themselves.

Left: With the scanty driver's seat covering removed, this shows just how basic the specification of the original Mini Moke actually was. No carpets, or trim pads, of course...

The 1965 Mini range

This was the total line-up of UK-market Minis with their retail prices:

Make and Model	Basic price	Total UK price with tax
Austin/Morris (850) Mini	£388	£469 15s 10d
Austin/Morris (850) Mini De Luxe	£425	£515 2s 1d
Austin/Morris Countryman/Traveller (steel)	£440	£532 12s 6d
Austin/Morris Countryman/Traveller (wood)	£456	£551 19s 2d
Austin/Morris Mini-Cooper (998cc)	£487	£590 0s 5d
Austin/Morris Mini-Cooper 970S	£573	£693 6s 8d
Austin/Morris Mini-Cooper 1275S	£643	£777 18s 4d
Riley Elf II (998cc)	£493	£596 13s 4d
Wolseley Hornet II (998cc)	£478	£578 10s 10d
Mini Moke (848cc)	£335	£406 7s 1d
For comparison only:		
Ford Anglia 105E	£395	£478 17s 1d
Hillman Imp	£420	£509 1s 3d
Vauxhall Viva HA	£436	£528 7s 11d

The 848cc Austin/Morris Mini van and pick-up were classed as commercial vehicles and did not attract purchase tax, so are not included in the car range above.

Perhaps because there was some disruption in phasing in Hydrolastic suspension but more likely because of the industrial problems which continually afflicted BMC at this time, total Mini production for 1965 (at Longbridge and Cowley) fell back slightly – 221,974 compared with 244,359 in 1964.

Rare at home

So, who would buy the Moke when it got on to the market? BMC was most anxious to find out. In theory, this was a car that should have appealed to country dwellers – or at least those who occasionally wanted to go scrabbling off metalled roads – but it didn't work out like that.

Let's be honest – a Moke was not ideal for use in a cool, wet, climate, for it had too many fundamental problems – it was too basic, too crude, too slow and too cold for British buyers.

In fact, BMC soon discovered that most Mokes were being sold to export markets where the sun shone and the rain stayed away. Holidaymakers in Bermuda and the West Indies loved scudding around the sun-kissed shores where sunburn was a bigger problem than keeping their feet dry. As for smallholders and small businessmen in Britain – they didn't buy the Moke at all.

Yet in the mid-1960s, in 'Swinging London' (as the magazines used to call it!), the Moke had a brief vogue. Flower power, mini-skirts, beads, droopy moustaches, and psychedelic paint jobs on Mokes all seemed to go together, which is why we saw most of them buzzing up and down the Kings Road but few outside city limits. All in all, 14,518 were produced in the UK.

Forget the weather, though, for a moment and remember the Moke's character. Here was a machine that virtually invented the phrase 'fun car' – for it was as nimble as a Mini saloon, with an even more cheeky character and the sort of front-end style that made almost everyone smile.

Much-modified Mokes – those with Crayford 'Surrey' tops and trim, or with changed body styles – were rarities but even more attractive. The problem was that, by definition, they were even more prone to rusting than ordinary Mini saloons and for them to stand a chance of surviving they had to be stored indoors. By the late 1970s many British-built cars had crumbled away, which explains why a lot of today's Mokes are of the more modern variety, built overseas.

Mokes built overseas

In 1966 the Mini Moke went into production in Australia, at BMC's Sydney plant, initially with the 998cc A-series engine. The warmer climate suited the Moke's character and it prospered – later versions having 13in wheels (for BMC's engineers had always left plenty of space inside the wheelarches), more ground clearance, and a 1,098cc engine. Later a single-carburettor 1,275cc engine was also offered.

As Australia's cheapest car, it sold respectably for some years, being exported to 82 countries (a limited number came to the UK, it seems), and no fewer than 26,142 cars were produced before the end came in 1981.

Moke assembly in Portugal began at about this time (originally using CKD kits from Australia, before the tooling was moved to that country), more seriously from 1983 with 13in wheels and a roll cage but after a financial upheaval yet another version started up in 1984/1985, this time with 12in wheels and a 998cc engine, plus

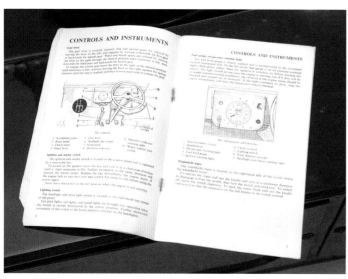

Top: This was how BMC hoped the Mini Moke would be seen, as a lightweight, fun-to-drive, working vehicle.

Above: Even though this was a limited-production machine, BMC provided a simple Instruction Book supplement, with all the necessary operational information.

Right: Is this a competition for 'how many people can a Mini-Moke carry'?

disc brakes. By this time, the structure was of galvanised steel, which helped to retard the onset of rusting.

The Moke then dropped out of production in 1989 but returned in 1991, still in Portugal but under new ownership by Cagiva of Italy. The last Portuguese cars were made in 1993, after no less than

10,060 such machines had been built. Although the press tools to make the bodyshell were then transferred to a new enterprise in Italy, production never got going again.

All in all, therefore, the Moke's career had lasted for 29 years, it had been built in three different countries, four different

A-series engines sizes had featured, and a total of 50,720 were sold. For an accountant, who could only read a balance sheet listing the investment cost of that unique hull, this must have made the project only marginally viable but as an image raiser the Moke was much more successful than that.

Specifications: Austin/Morris Mini Moke (UK assembly) 1964−1968

ENGINE

Description
In-line four-cylinder with cast iron block and cylinder head. Chain-driven camshaft in block, pushrod-operated overhead valves. Heart-shaped combustion chambers. Aluminium alloy pistons, forged steel connecting rods. Three-bearing counterweighted crankshaft

Capacity
848cc (51.8cu in)

Bore and stroke
62.94mm x 68.26mm (2.48in x 2.68in)

Compression ratio
8.3:1

Maximum power
34bhp @ 5,500rpm

Maximum torque
44lb ft (59Nm) @ 2,900rpm

Carburettor
Single 1¼in SU HS2

TRANSMISSION

Gearbox
Four-speed with synchromesh on top three gears

Ratios
1st	3.627:1
2nd	2.171:1
3rd	1.414:1
Top	1.000:1
Reverse	3.627:1

Clutch
Borg and Beck, 7¼in Single dry plate (diaphragm spring from late 1964)

Final drive
Helical spur gears, ratio: 3.44:1

BRAKES

Front
Lockheed drum, 7in x 1¼in

Rear
Lockheed drum, 7in x 1¼in

Operation
Lockheed hydraulic

Handbrake
Lever, with cable linkage to rear drums

SUSPENSION

Front
Independent, rubber cone springs, double wishbones, telescopic dampers

Rear
Independent, rubber cone springs, trailing arms, telescopic dampers

STEERING

Type
Rack and pinion

Number of turns lock to lock
2¾

Turning circle
32ft 0in (9.75m) approx, between kerbs

Steering wheel
Two spoke, 15¾in diameter

WHEELS AND TYRES
3½J x 10in steel disc wheels

Tyres
5.20-10in cross-ply

PERFORMANCE

Top speed
65mph (104kph)

Acceleration
0–30mph (48kph)	6.2sec
0–50mph (80kph)	15.4sec
0–60mph (96kph)	21.8sec
Standing quarter mile (402m)	23.3sec

Overall fuel consumption
40.1mpg (7.0l/100km)

DIMENSIONS

Length
10ft 0in (3,048mm)

Width
4ft 3½in (1,308mm)

Height
4ft 8in (1,422mm)

Wheelbase
6ft 8⅛in (2,036mm)

Track
Front: 3ft 11⅜in (1,203mm)
Rear: 3ft 9⅞in (1,165mm)

Ground Clearance
7⅛in (181mm)

Unladen weight
1,176lb (533kg)

Twini-Moke

Perhaps it was only a publicity stunt but at Longbridge the appearance of a twin-engined Moke during the Arctic winter of 1963 made many headlines. At the time, BMC said this was a serious project but I doubt if it ever made economic sense.

To provide a four-wheel-drive, go-nearly-anywhere, Moke, Issigonis's designers took a normal Moke, grafted a complete front subframe, 848cc engine and transmission under the rear of the platform hull, made sure that the steering arms were firmly fixed in the straight-ahead position, and arranged a complex and rather willowy

Below: Minis came in many forms during the 1960s but the vast majority were simple 848cc-engined models. Nearly 200,000 such cars were built in 1965.

gear change linkage along the side of the hull to a right-hand gear lever. The two engine/transmission power packs shared the same clutch hydraulics but there was only one clutch and they were otherwise not connected.

Thus (wrote Pomeroy): 'Double de-clutching took on a new significance – that when starting from rest, one engaged second gear first at one end of the car and then at the other end...'

On very slippery surfaces – and if you were brave and skilful – one could run with different gears engaged at each

end of the car, which did mysterious things to tyre slip angles and handling characteristics. Entertaining but not recommended...

In sporting terms, BMC was serious about this derivative for a time – twin 1100-engined versions were tested and similar twin-engined racing Mini-Coopers were also developed – but the idea didn't get very far. With expensive engines and transmissions filling the front and rear areas of the chassis, there was nowhere to put, or carry, loads and the project was soon abandoned.

Range changes for 1966

As already noted, from October 1965 Automotive Products automatic transmission was made optional on 848cc-engined Austin and Morris Mini saloons – but not on any other of the derivatives – which took up most of BMC's new-product activity at the Earls Court Motor Show. Even then, automatic transmission was not generally available in any numbers until mid-1966, for the launch had been somewhat premature.

Upgrading the 1275S

By the end of 1965, both the Mini-Cooper 1071S and Mini-Cooper 970S models had been dropped, which left the 1275S as the only 'S' model in production. At the time, its engine was unique, in that no other BMC model was currently using it, though plans were already laid to productionise it, de-tune it, and make it available in other cars in the BMC range.

Although Hydrolastic suspension had been standardised from late 1964, AP automatic transmission was not (and never would be) made available as an option on that model. However, other, unique, modifications were on the way.

Early in 1966 (and not unconnected with improvements demanded by the works motor sport department at Abingdon), the 1275S became the only Mini to have twin fuel tanks as standard – 5½ gallons on each side of the boot,

which did nothing for the carrying capacity – and at the same time an engine oil cooler (placed forward, in a cooling stream of air through the nose) was also made standard.

A few months later (April 1966), the chassis was also uprated, with higher-rate Hydrolastic units, heavy-duty front lower-wishbone bushes, solid universal joints in the driveshafts, taper-roller rear hub bearings, and extra stiffening for the suspension mountings. All these had been found necessary in the rough and tumble of International motor sport – and all would help the 1275S add a remarkable number of victories in the next two seasons.

Left: Nice compliment to the Mini-Cooper S but was it cheating? Certain police forces used these amazing little cars in the mid-1960s. But where did they put all the cones, notice boards, and banners...?

The Mini-Cooper 1275S and its rivals in 1964

Make and model	Top speed	0–60mph	Standing ¼ mile	Fuel consumption	Price inc tax
Austin-Healy Sprite	91mph	14.5sec	19.4sec	30mpg	£622
Ford Cortina GT	93mph	13.9sec	18.7sec	26mpg	£825
Ford Cortina-Lotus	107mph	9.9sec	17.4sec	21mpg	£1,028
Mini-Cooper (998cc)	90mph	16.8sec	20.1sec	33mpg	£600
Mini-Cooper 1275S	96mph	11.2sec	18.4sec	29mpg	£791
Renault 8 Gordini	106mph	12.3sec	18.8sec	25mpg	£1,001
Sunbeam Imp Sport	90mph	16.3sec	20.2sec	33mpg	£665

Below: Abingdon's 'works' competitions workshops were always busy, especially in the run up to the Monte Carlo Rally, when, by tradition, brand-new cars were often used.

Mini-Cooper in motor sport: a winning streak

Between 1964 and 1967 the 1275S became the most successful competition car in Europe. No matter how rivals tried to measure success in another manner, the fact is that front-wheel-drive Minis won more races and rallies than any of their rivals. Whether these were 'works' rally cars, 'works-backed' racecars, or often if they were well-prepared and supported privately-owned cars, a Mini could keep up with, and often defeat, some of the most powerful competition cars in Europe.

'Works' rally cars

To get an idea of just how remarkable the well-developed and beautifully prepared cars from Abingdon had become, it is necessary to refer to the table of successes on page 80. This shows that, after 1964

Cooper S major rally victories 1965–1967

1965	Monte (Timo Makinen)	Cooper S 1,275cc
	Circuit of Ireland (Paddy Hopkirk)	Cooper S 1,275cc
	Geneva (Rauno Aaltonen)	Cooper S 1,275cc
	Czech (Rauno Aaltonen)	Cooper S 1,275cc
	Polish (Rauno Aaltonen)	Cooper S 1,275cc
	1000 Lakes (Timo Makinen)	Cooper S 1,275cc
	Three Cities (Rauno Aaltonen)	Cooper S 1,275cc
	RAC (Rauno Aaltonen)	Cooper S 1,275cc
1966	Monte (Timo Makinen)	Cooper S 1,275cc*
	Circuit of Ireland (Tony Fall)	Cooper S 1,275cc
	Tulip (Rauno Aaltonen)	Cooper S 1,275cc
	Austrian Alpine (Paddy Hopkirk)	Cooper S 1,275cc
	Scottish (Tony Fall)	Cooper S 1,275cc
	Czech (Rauno Aaltonen)	Cooper S 1,275cc
	Polish (Tony Fall)	Cooper S 1,275cc
	1000 Lakes (Timo Makinen)	Cooper S 1,275cc
	Three Cities (Timo Makinen)	Cooper S 1,275cc
1967	Monte (Rauno Aaltonen)	Cooper S 1,275cc
	Circuit of Ireland (Paddy Hopkirk)	Cooper S 1,275cc
	Acropolis (Paddy Hopkirk)	Cooper S 1,275cc
	Geneva (Tony Fall)	Cooper S 1,275cc
	1000 Lakes (Timo Makinen)	Cooper S 1,275cc
	French Alpine (Paddy Hopkirk)	Cooper S 1,275cc

* Disqualified after the event, on a headlamp operation technicality

Top right: Service at the roadside for one of the 'works' Mini-Cooper S types, which were Europe's most successful rally cars in the mid-1960s. Quick-lift jacks were just one of the innovations that the Abingdon team developed in those years.

Right: Granted 'Number 1' for the 1964 RAC Rally, in recognition of their famous Monte victory, Paddy Hopkirk and Henry Liddon start the rally from London. CRX 90B looked, and was, brand new for that event.

when the 1275S had come on stream and after the team had learned how to super-tune the engines and to keep the much-improved transmissions in one piece, then this was an incredibly capable machine.

By 1965, when Abingdon had brought a rival sports car, the Austin-Healey 3000, to the peak of its development, it was astonishing, but true, to see that the 1275S could often outpace that car. The 'Big Healey' (as it was always affectionately known) was certainly faster on tarmac stages, or on a racetrack, but the fully developed 1275S was often faster on all but the roughest of loose-surface special stages. Not only that but if it broke, mechanics found that they could repair it faster and more effectively than the Healey.

Even so, Abingdon had to treat these cars as consumables, for in the hands of their superstar drivers – Paddy Hopkirk, Timo Makinen, Rauno Aaltonen, and Tony Fall – they were usually driven so hard that they took a terribly battering. Between 1964 and 1967, fleets of Mini-Cooper S types were prepared and re-prepared to do battle. Peter Browning's excellent book *The Works Minis* shows that no fewer than 37 brand new, and different, identities (by registration number) were employed. Not only that but (as is well known) any rally car which had a particularly hard time was re-shelled more than once. I have no doubt that more than 100 different 'cars' were used in that period. Sometimes, more than one example of a particular 'identity' is claimed to have survived – and both latter-day owners may have a point.

Over time, incidentally, there seemed to be no settled policy to cover the use of Austin or Morris identities. Along with the geographic choice of some events, this sometimes depended on the influence and importance of the importer or dealer chain in that country. Some 'works' cars changed their badge identities at least once during their lives and there are recorded instances of matters being in such chaos that Austin and Morris badging (at front, rear, and on the steering wheel horn button) both appeared on the same car, at the same time, on the same event.

Except on very rare occasions (when there was particular kudos, or valuable class and financial bonuses to be gained), the 970S was not used in rallying. Once the last of the 997cc Mini-Coopers had been pensioned off, almost every Abingdon entry was of a 1275S. Although it was BMC marketing policy to push the merits of Hydrolastic ('wet') suspension at this time, a surprising number of these 'works' Minis were still used in old-style rubber ('dry') form, or had suitable screw-down taps placed out of sight, under the rear seat cushion, so that the fore-aft transfer of Hydrolastic fluid could be stopped.

As with the policy on badging (mentioned above), a 'works' car might be 'wet' at one point of its career and 'dry' at another, for both layouts were homologated and there was no important packaging problem in swapping one system for the other. A driver's own preferences were always taken into account when cars were being prepared or allocated – and since there was no such thing as a dedicated 'Paddy' or 'Timo' car, this could make preparation and re-preparation even more complex.

Left: Business end! GRX 195D was one of the fleet of 'works' rally cars prepared at Abingdon in the 1960s. Timo Makinen drove this car to win the Finnish 1000 Lakes Rally of 1967.

Below: Paddy Hopkirk and Henry Liddon, pushing on in their 'works' 1275S rally car, in the 1965 Scottish Rally.

Meeting the rally regulations

Rally regulations, too, had an influence on how a car was prepared. Some events (like the notorious Monte of 1966) were run for 'Group 1' (showroom standard) machines, which meant that very few improvements were allowed. Others ran to 'Group 2' rules, where all the team's homologated extras, including 100/110bhp-plus engines, straight-cut gearboxes, Minilite wheels, special seats, and a host more pieces, could all be employed.

Where there was any advantage to be gained, the same cars might be entered in Group 3 (Grand Touring) or even in Group 6 (Prototype) guise, where exotic and non-homologated items such as aluminium or glass-fibre body panels and Perspex side and rear windows could all be employed, and where surplus weight could be pared away ruthlessly. For all these reasons, therefore, it is quite impossible to respond to the question: 'What goes into a "works"

Mini?' – and it also makes it difficult to identify or authenticate the hulk of a neglected old 'barn find' that may be claimed as a long-lost/now-discovered 'works' rally car.

Some of the famous victories have become legendary among Mini fans – Monte Carlo in 1965 and 1967 being perfect examples – but Timo Makinen's disqualification from the 1966 event (after he had won it 'on the road') also has its own corner in the Mini Hall of Fame. That was an occasion when the organisers were widely accused of favouring French cars to win the 'showroom' category event which had been devised, and when the scrutineers clutched at any straw (in this case single filament quartz-iodine headlamp bulbs) to make sure that the Minis were excluded.

Each and every superstar driver won several major International events outright, though it was only Rauno

'Works-supported' race cars

After the 1964 European Saloon Car Championship success, Abingdon's contracted teams found themselves coming under more and more pressure from 'homologation specials' that had been introduced by their rivals: such cars, whether in the Mini-Cooper classes or not, were also built with class domination in mind and often had very different engines from their standard relatives.

For that reason, Abingdon concentrated on the British series, with occasional forays to important overseas events. This explains why three 'works' cars were sent out to Sebring, in Florida, in March 1965, where Warwick Banks/Paddy Hopkirk (whose car had fuel feed problems) finished closely behind a class-winning ex-Broadspeed car.

In Britain, in 1965, the Cooper Car Co cars were driven by John Rhodes (1,300cc class) and Warwick Banks (1,000cc class), their main class opposition coming from the privately financed Broadspeed machines (driven by John Fitzpatrick and John Handley). After a ding-dong battle with the Superspeed 1.3-litre Ford Anglias, Rhodes won his class, while Banks easily won the 1-litre category and took second place overall in the series. This was a season, incidentally, when the Broadspeed cars sometimes proved to be faster than the Cooper Car Co machines, which was embarrassing. The situation did not persist into 1966 as Broadspeed defected, to campaign Ford Anglias instead!

For 1966, under pressure from manufacturers rival to BMC, the BRSCC changed its Championship regulations completely. Henceforth the racing would be under FIA Group 5 regulations, which was effectively a free formula, in that the original bodyshell and the original engine cylinder block had to be retained but almost everything else could be changed. This meant that poorly specified cars like the Ford Anglia Super could benefit enormously, while well-developed road cars like the 1275S had little to gain.

In 1966, as it happens, the 1,300cc class featured a season-long points battle between John Rhodes's Cooper Car Co 1275S and John Fitzpatrick's 1-litre Broadspeed Ford

aaltonen who was suitably stage-managed by BMC to win the European Rally Championship of 1965, with five outright victories in that season alone. Timo Makinen was widely accepted as the world's fastest driver in this period but was also hardest on his cars, which explains the number of retirements. Rauno Aaltonen, on the other hand, was the most analytical and would sketch out desired modifications to his car on any white surface available – on one famous occasion, this was the white tablecloth of a restaurant where he was having dinner!

The 'works' Minis deserved to win more than one RAC Rally (Aaltonen in 1965 –

defeating Makinen's Healey 3000 in a straight fight on snowy stages) and deserved to win more than two French Alpines (Paddy's win in 1967 was a famous victory in a Group 6 car), though it was surely asking too much for Aaltonen to tackle the 1967 Safari in a 1275S (a car supplied complete with its own on-board pump-up kit for the Hydrolastic suspension)?

During his time at Abingdon, it was team boss Stuart Turner who helped bring these cars to the peak of their powers; when he moved on in January 1967, it was Peter Browning who so capably took over until the last-ever 'works' Minis were rallied in 1970.

Left: The British Motor Industry Heritage Trust was proud to look after three famous 'works' 1275S types, after they had won the Monte Carlo Rally, and displayed them imaginatively, like this. Left to right: 33 EJB was the 1964 winner, LBL 6D won in 1967, and AJB 44B took the honours in 1965.

Left: If Rauno Aaltonen had not won a sponsored entry for the 1967 East African Safari, he would surely never have taken this Mini to grapple with the mud and dust of Kenya? Fitted with onboard pump-up equipment for the Hydrolastic suspension, with extra driving lamps close to the windscreen, and lifting handles at all four corners, the gallant little car did its best but could not quite cope with primitive conditions in the bush.

Elf and Hornet MkIIIs

In the previous chapter, I have already noted that in 1963 the Riley Elf/Wolseley Hornet models were the first of the Mini family to be fitted with 998cc engines: as with all other Mini saloons, too, they were equipped with Hydrolastic suspension and diaphragm spring clutches from the autumn of 1964.

BMC also announced further-developed Riley Elf and Wolseley Hornet saloons, this time in MkIII guise, in the autumn of 1966. Revealed on the very eve of the Earls Court Motor Show, these took the Elf/Hornet twins another clear step ahead of other Minis. Although there were no significant mechanical changes – the 38bhp/998cc engine and the Hydrolastic suspension were as before – it was the body that had been altered.

These therefore became the first UK-market Minis to use wind-up windows in the doors (Australian-market Minis had been fitted with a different type a year earlier, however), these doors henceforth having concealed hinges. Inside the cabin, swivelling 'eyeball' fresh-air vents were fitted to each side of the facia and the Mini Cooper type of stubby, remote-control gear change was also standardised.

This was still not the end of their development, for the Elf/Hornet cars invariably picked up improvements being made to other Minis, though sometimes n͏͏ at the same juncture: once again, these are described more fully in the next chapter.

Above: John 'Smoking' Rhodes was the fastest of all Mini-Cooper S racing drivers and was the team leader of the 'works' John Cooper team in the British Saloon Car Championship in the mid-1960s.

Top right: The final derivation of the Wolseley Hornet retained this Mini-Cooper-like instrument layout and the remote-control gearshift, along with face-level ventilation. In the passenger doors, the definitive wind-up window installation is just visible.

Right: Production of the Wolseley Hornet (and its sister, the Riley Elf) carried on steadily in the mid-1960s, latterly in MkIII form, complete with wind-up windows and a 998cc engine.

Anglia. At the end of that year, both cars ended up with the same number of points at the head of the listings but the 1275S, still with a twin-choke Weber carburettor (instead of twin SUs) and about 120bhp from its Downton-tuned power unit, was clearly close to the peak of its development in that form.

By this time, Rhodes's driving methods (which seemed to be to ignore the brake pedal almost completely, to throw the car sideways before the corner, to lay a dense smoke screen from the spinning front wheels as he negotiated the corner, and to blind his rivals) were becoming legendary. Nothing that Dunlop could do would reduce the tyre smoke – but as Rhodes only wanted a cover to last for about one hour of racing, he wasn't at all worried about tyre wear...

A year later, Rhodes was retaining his mastery of the 1.3-litre class, helped along by the use of Lucas fuel injection instead of a carburettor, though with the Group 5 Superspeed Anglias now developing about 145bhp this was beginning to be a real struggle. Even so, he triumphed by sheer consistency, won his capacity class, and took third overall in the Championship.

For 1968, though, it really would be 'deep-breath' time, for Broadspeed was expected to be running new, state-of-the-art Escort 1300s...

Stability – with change on the way

By 1966 and 1967, seasoned BMC watchers could see that the Mini's range and specifications were settling down, though in fairness to BMC's engineers and planners, they had been very busy indeed in other directions – notably in developing more and yet more 1100 derivatives, in feeding in the first detuned 1,275cc-engined 1100s on to the market, and in bringing the large, front-wheel-drive 1800 into the showrooms.

As far as the Mini was concerned, howev͏ very little other innovation had followed t͏ launch of the automatic transmission opti͏ This, the watchers, concluded, meant that something new was being planned. They were right. First in 1967, and then in 1969, the Mini was about to be rejigged.

Specifications: Mini-Cooper 1275S, 1964–1967

ENGINE

Description
In-line four-cylinder with cast iron block and cylinder head. Chain-driven camshaft in block, pushrod-operated overhead valves. Heart-shaped combustion chambers. Aluminium alloy pistons, forged steel connecting rods. Three-bearing counter-weighted crankshaft

Capacity
1,275cc (77.8cu in)

Bore and stroke
70.64mm x 81.33mm (2.78in x 3.20in)

Compression ratio
9.75:1

Maximum power
76bhp @ 5,800rpm

Maximum torque
79lb ft (107Nm) @ 3,000rpm

Carburettor
Two 1¼in SU HS2

TRANSMISSION

Gearbox
Four-speed with synchromesh on top three gears

Ratios	Standard	Close ratio
1st	3.198:1	2.565:1
2nd	1.915:1	1.780:1
3rd	1.354:1	1.240:1
Top	1.000:1	1.000:1
Reverse	3.198:1	2.565:1

Clutch
Borg and Beck, 7⅛in diaphragm spring

Final drive
Helical spur gears, ratio: 3.44:1 (optional 3.765:1)

BRAKES

Front
Lockheed disc, 7½in

Rear
Lockheed drum, 7in x 1¼in

Operation
Lockheed hydraulic, with vacuum servo assistance

Handbrake
Lever, with cable linkage to rear drums

SUSPENSION

Front
Independent, rubber cone springs (Hydrolastic suspension units, with hydraulic connection to rear suspension, from late 1964), double wishbones, telescopic dampers

Rear
Independent, rubber cone springs (Hydrolastic suspension units, with hydraulic connection to front suspension, from late 1964), trailing arms, telescopic dampers

STEERING

Type
Rack and pinion

Number of turns lock to lock
2⅓

Turning circle
32ft 0in (9.75m) approx, between kerbs

Steering wheel
Two-spoke, 15¾in diameter

WHEELS AND TYRES
3½J x 10in steel disc wheels (optional 4½J wheels at first, standard from late 1965)

Tyres
145-10in radial-ply

PERFORMANCE
Autocar road test, 14 August 1964

Top speed
96mph (154kph)

Acceleration

0–30mph (48kph)	3.5sec
0–50mph (80kph)	8.2sec
0–60mph (96kph)	11.2sec
0–70mph (112kph)	15.4sec
0–80mph (128kph)	23.4sec
0–90mph (144kph)	34.7sec
Standing quarter mile (402m)	18.4sec

Overall fuel consumption
28.5mpg (9.9l/100km)

DIMENSIONS

Length
10ft 0¼in (3,054mm)

Width
4ft 7in (1,397mm)

Height
4ft 5in (1,346mm)

Wheelbase
6ft 8³²/₃₂in (2,036mm)

Track
Front: 3ft 11½in (1,207mm)
Rear: 3ft 10⁵/₁₆in (1,176mm)

Ground Clearance
6in (152mm)

Unladen weight
1,535lb (696kg)

MINI MKII, MKIII, CLUBMAN & INNOCENTI 1967–1990

1967–1990
The MkII update and 'Mini' becomes a marque

Although this book covers the fortunes of just one famous car, it must also reflect the fortunes of the company that was building it. To understand why and how the Mini changed in the late 1960s, it is also important to know about BMC's financial fortunes at this time.

Not only was BMC regularly afflicted by unofficial strike action at its own factories but by the vicissitudes of its major suppliers. Not only did this lead to a loss of output, and therefore a loss of sales, but it also led to a loss of profit – and this meant that investment in future models often had to be cut back to suit.

In corporate terms, it did not help that BMC was also having to digest two recent mergers – the takeover of Pressed Steel in 1965 and of Jaguar (plus Daimler, Coventry-Climax, Guy and Meadows) in 1966. The result was the foundation of British Motor Holdings (BMH), a new conglomerate, which was going to take time to settle down.

No finance to replace the Mini

Although Alec Issigonis, his engineers and the stylists knew what they wanted to do, not only to keep on improving the Mini but eventually to replace it, the lack of profit usually made this impossible. In 1965, BMC's profit (after tax) was £16.3 million, in 1966 it was £15.1 million, but in 1967 it fell to only £3.9 million. Although BMC put a brave face on those figures, the fact is that they were inadequate. Because investment had to be spread over several models, the Mini was no longer an immediate priority. The major spending in 1967 was going into the new Austin Maxi and its brand-new engine, the new Austin 3-Litre, and into the retooling of the A-series and C-series, which powered the Mini and 3-Litre respectively.)

Although Alec Issigonis's current master plan envisaged a completely new range of small overhead-camshaft four-cylinder and six-cylinder engines, and a brand-new Mini-replacement model coded 9X, the capital to put those new products into production was simply not available.

Accordingly, the next step in the evolution of the Mini range was neither to replace it, nor to bring in major updates but to bring in a series of what were once called 'major-minor' changes instead. This occurred in two stages – first by the creation of the short-lived MkII, the second by the introduction of the ADO20/MkIII type.

MkII Minis: reworking wherever possible

By 1967 the Mini was approaching its eighth birthday. Companies which were making more money, and which had more aggressive marketing policies (Ford was a perfect example), would want to introduce a completely new model by this point but BMC simply could not afford it. Body press tools and facilities laid down in 1959 had already produced one-and-a-half million bodies from three different sources and some were in urgent need of replacement.

At the same time, much work had gone into the evolution of the A-series engine. When the Mini had been new, only 848cc and 948cc capacities had been available but by 1965 there were 848cc, 970cc,

998cc, 1,098cc, and 1,275cc sizes. This, also, was a time for rationalisation and retooling on a big scale – and the Mini would benefit from that change.

In October 1967, therefore, BMC announced what it called the MkII range of Minis – this applying to every snub-nosed type (saloon, estate car, van, or pick-up) but not to the Riley Elf and Wolseley Hornet, which had been updated in their own way in 1966.

Despite spending only a minimum amount on new press tools, BMC had made significant changes to the bodyshell and the styling differences were clear from all angles. At the front , the grilles had been

reprofiled and slightly enlarged (Austin and Morris models still retained their own, individual, styles), while at the rear the back window had been slightly widened, and there was a new, larger, type of tail lamp. There was also new badging at front and rear.

Inside the cars, the Basic model was much as before but the Super de Luxe types now had the three-dial (Mini-Cooper type) instrument cluster, restyled and (BMC claimed) more comfortable seats, and the remote-control gear change, which had been seen first in Mini-Coopers (and, more recently, in the Elf and Hornet twins).

Above: Posed in the gardens in the centre of Longbridge (that is 'The Kremlin', BMC's main administrative block, in the background) the 1968-model Super de Luxe MkII shows only minor visual differences over the MkI, noticeably the larger front grille.

Opposite: MkII estate car derivatives were available with or without the 'woody' fittings – this being the all-steel version.

Mechanically, on the Super de Luxe the big improvement on the saloons, vans, and pick-ups was the choice between 34bhp/848cc and 38bhp/998cc engines. The Countryman/Traveller estate cars adopted the 998cc engine as standard. Larger engines were also mated to the higher (Cooper S-type) 3.44:1 final drive ratio and AP's four-speed automatic transmission was still optional on both types. Within weeks a plastic cooling fan was also standardised.

One important change to the chassis was that a revised rack-and-pinion steering assembly, allied to lengthened steering arms, helped to reduce the already tight turning circle from 32ft to only 28ft. The original Mini had always been manoeuvrable but the latest variety was even more so.

From this point on, therefore, there wer no fewer than eight different Austin/Morris Mini derivatives in the line-up:

Austin/Morris Mini 850
Austin/Morris Mini 850 Super de Luxe
Austin/Morris Mini 1000 Super de Luxe
Austin Mini Countryman/Morris Mini
    Traveller (998cc as standard)
Austin/Morris Mini 850 van
Austin/Morris Mini 1000 van
Austin/Morris Mini 850 pick-up
Austin/Morris Mini 1000 pick-up

For the next few weeks, incidentally, Mir MkIIs would be built at Longbridge and at Cowley, though the Mini assembly line at Cowley would finally close down (to make space for the forthcoming Austin Maxi) in January 1968.

MkII Mini-Coopers

Cooper-badged Minis also became MkII at the same time as the mass-market Minis, though by this time only the 998cc Mini-Cooper and the 1,275cc Mini-Cooper S were available. Bodyshell changes were all shared with the mass-market cars, though from this moment on both Austin and Morris shared the same style of radiator grille (which had seven horizontal chrome bars). Now the only difference between the two marques was in the badging – at this

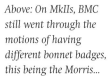

Above: On MkIIs, BMC still went through the motions of having different bonnet badges, this being the Morris...

Right: ...but common boot emblems.

The Mini 1000 MkII and its rivals in October 1967

Make and model	Top speed	0–60mph	Standing ¼ mile	Fuel consumption	Price inc tax
Fiat 850S	76mph	26.8sec	22.9sec	35mpg	£559
Ford Anglia De Luxe	76mph	29.4sec	23.0sec	36mpg	£596
Hillman Imp De Luxe	81mph	23.7sec	21.8sec	38mpg	£567
Honda N600	82mph	18.3sec	21.1sec	35mpg	£510
Mini 1000 Super de Luxe	75mph	26.2sec	22.7sec	34mpg	£579
NSU Prinz 4L	72mph	27.7sec	23.6sec	37mpg	£584
Renault 4L	66mph	38.1sec	24.6sec	37mpg	£559
Simca 1000LS	78mph	22.5sec	21.8sec	32mpg	£619
Skoda 1000MB De Luxe	75mph	30.8sec	23.6sec	31mpg	£600
Volkswagen 1200 Beetle	71mph	27.5sec	22.9sec	31mpg	£595
Wolseley Hornet III	77mph	24.1sec	22.4sec	35mpg	£629

Left: Although the Mini-Cooper S was the more glamorous type, it was this car, the 998cc Mini-Cooper MkII, which sold much better. Badged as an Austin, and with Dunlop radial-ply tyres, this was a very popular, and familiar, car on British roads.

Far left: Compared with the earlier MkI types, for 1968 the revised MkII Mini-Cooper S featured a larger rear window and new badges. The twin fuel tanks had been standard since the beginning of 1966.

Left: Emphasising the British-by-Gad character of the Mini-Cooper S, BMC made sure that London's Houses of Parliament, was in shot with this MkII.

Right: Although MkII Mini-Cooper S models did not all have duotone body colour, they were all built with twin fuel tanks and radial-ply tyres and came complete with a different front grille and a new bonnet badge.

time it was not unknown for 'works' competition cars to appear on the start-line of events with an unplanned mixture of front and rear badges! Mechanically there was little change compared with the last of the MkIs – the power output of the 1275S, for instance, never moved from its original rating of 76bhp at 5,800rpm – though the Cooper S would be the first to benefit from the new all-synchromesh gearbox during 1968. The last of the MkII Cooper S models would be built at the end of 1969, though the replacement ADO20-type MkIII would not go on sale until March 1970.

New gearboxes and rising production

Although the arrival of an all-synchromesh four-speed transmission was first mentioned by BMC before the end of 1967, this was yet

Right: This is the underbonnet layout of a Mini-Cooper 1275S MkII, complete with vacuum brake servo and, on this particular car, larger-than-normal SU carburettors.

Opposite: From late 1967, the Mini-Cooper 1275S had a modified nose, with an enlarged grille aperture. From this point, too, Austin and Morris Coopers shared the same grille style.

another BMC/British Leyland launch which was premature, to say the least. In the event, all-synchromesh gears (with the same internal ratios as the original types) were introduced gradually during 1968, the process not being complete on all models – Mini, Mini-Cooper, Cooper S, Riley Elf, and Wolseley Hornet – until October 1968. That, in fact, was the last change that would be made to that gearbox-in-sump installation for the next quarter of a century.

For the entire Mini range, 1968 was not only the year in which British Leyland was formed (by the merger of British Motor Holdings and the Leyland Group) but the year in which Alec Issigonis's influence on technical developments – most especially on the improvement of the Mini – was terminated. His still unauthorised Mini-replacement project (coded 9X) was frozen out and what was now called Austin-Morris turned its attention to further developments of the existing Mini pedigree.

Production of MkII Minis positively boomed. In 1967 Mini (MkI and MkII) output had been 237,227 but in 1968 it rose to 246,066 and would increase again in 1969 to no fewer than 254,957. This was a record (so far) for Mini production, yet that figure would soon be surpassed.

Annual production would peak at 318,475 in 1971, then gradually began to decline.

Above: For 1968, the Mini-Cooper S MkII facia/instrument panel display was virtually the same as that already familiar on 1964–1967 models.

Late-model Riley Elf and Wolseley Hornet

In October 1967 the ingeniously-packaged four-speed AP automatic transmission became optional at a cost of £92 on Elf and Hornet models: this had been optional on Austin/Morris Minis since late 1965. This price may not sound much but in 1967 that was a 15 per cent impost (today's equivalent price would be about £1,300–£1,400) – which explains why not many were ordered!

In summer 1968 (August is quoted in service literature but in truth this was a rather long drawn-out introduction) the latest type of BMC all-synchromesh gearbox finally took over from the original type of box. The existence of this box had been revealed in the autumn of 1967 but it was altogether typical of BMC (soon to be British Leyland) that supplies were not immediately available.

No sooner had British Leyland come into existence (formally, that is, in May 1968), than the new management team began to prune the various ranges – the unique-bodied Elf and Hornet were among the first to come under scrutiny. Since they were only being made at a rate of about 500 cars a month, based on a bodyshell which was awkward, and unique, to construct, they were obvious targets for cancellation.

In the autumn of 1969, therefore – and just ahead of the arrival of the wind-up window British Minis – the Elf and Hornet models were killed off. In fact, this was also the end of Riley, though not yet for Wolseley, which would live on in larger-model guise until 1975.

Throughout their lives, these cars had a particular marketing image – exactly the one BMC planners had always intended for them. They were the best equipped and most completely specified of all the Minis, though because they were slightly heavier, they were actually a little slower than the Austin/Morris models.

Killing off the Mini-Cooper

Almost at the same time as the Elf and Hornet models were killed off, British Leyland also decided to cancel the Mini-Cooper (though not the Mini-Cooper S). This, at least, would be done cleanly, immediately in advance of the launch of the much-changed wind-up-window ADO20 models.

Official figures show that between 12,000 and 14,000 Mini-Coopers were being produced every year in the mid-1960s. When the model was cancelled, British Leyland made much of the fact that this represented only five per cent of total Mini production and that certain features – front-wheel disc brakes and the 998cc twin-carburettor engine for instance – were unique to this model but the real reason for the cancellation was more mundane.

No sooner had he taken charge at Longbridge than Sir Donald (later Lord) Stokes ordered a cull of consultants and of royalty payments to those like Cooper and Healey whose names were attached to one of 'his' cars. His team, he was assured, could do just as well without their help and at no extra cost. Its first 'low-cost' effort, as we shall see in the next chapter, was to develop the long-nose single-carburettor Mini 1275GT.

Accordingly, Daniel Richmond (whose cylinder head/breathing expertise had proved to be invaluable to the engineering team) was speedily cast adrift, while Donald Healey was put under notice, as was John Cooper.

Mini-Cooper, but not Cooper S, assembly therefore ran down in the autumn of 1969 and ended ahead of the changeover to 'ADO20' Mini bodyshells taking place. If the Mini-Cooper S had not been such an on-going success in motor sport, that model also might have been killed off in 1969 but in fact it would be reborn in wind-up window form – theoretically in November 1969 but actually in March 1970. All in all, 64,224 MkI Mini-Coopers had been built, along with (since late 1967) 16,396 MkIIs – a grand total of 80,620 cars. In spite of what a killjoy cost accountant might try to prove, this must have been a highly profitable project – and John Cooper thoroughly deserved every royalty that he was granted.

Mini-Cooper S in motor sport

When British Motor Holdings merged with Leyland Motors in January 1968, to form British Leyland, Abingdon could have had no idea of the huge impact this would have on its race and rallying activities. Soon after the merger was formalised, British Leyland set out on a rationalisation programme and it was made clear that all the corporation's marques – including Rover and Triumph – should be considered for future motor sport programmes.

Fortunately for Peter Browning and the Cooper Car Co, by the time this edict came down, plans for the 1968 season were already in place. It was pure coincidence, however, that this was the year in which the 1275S was gradually overhauled by new opposition, principally from Ford. In 1969, with British Leyland's antipathy to competing anywhere in which it could not almost guarantee success, all 'works' programmes would be slashed.

Although there were no more outright wins to celebrate in 1968, the 1275S was still ultra-competitive. Third on the Monte (Aaltonen), third on the Tulip (Vernaeve), and second on the Scottish (Ytterbring) all proved this but with Abingdon concentrating on preparing 1800s for the Safari and the London–Sydney Marathon, this was a restricted programme.

Apart from Paddy Hopkirk's second overall in the Circuit of Ireland in 1969, and a fine class win in the Tour de France,

there would be no 'works' entries at all. Lord Stokes's advisers made sure that Abingdon committed itself to racing and rallycross, where the crowds were larger and the expenses were reduced.

Invented in the late 1960s to help TV fill its schedules on wet Saturday afternoons, rallycross – a cross between autocross (cars competing on loose surfaces on their own) and racing (small grids, on mixed surfaces) – had soon become very popular. Where traction and handling mattered, stripped-out 1275S types (driven by heroes like Hugh Wheldon and 'Jumping Jeff' Williamson) soon became common.

As part of Lord Stokes's 'win where the public can see you doing it' policy, Abingdon was directed to enter cars in the ITV winter series of 1968/1969. Handicapped by a total lack of preparation experience at first, the team provided John Rhodes and John Handley with ever-improving cars. The first victory came in April 1969 and in the end Rhodes's consistency provided second overall in the Championship series but this was an experiment that was not repeated in the future.

In 1968 the Cooper Car Co ran the 'official' 1275S race team (John Rhodes and Steve Neal were the drivers), while there was also support for John Handley's British Vita-prepared 970S in the European Championship.

Left: Was this the original Maxi-Mini? Just for show, you understand, and if you look closely you will see how two cars and some extra panelling turned this into an eye-catching showroom exhibit!

This was the point at which Lord Stokes withdrew all financial support from contracted teams and from Downton Engineering. Not only was Abingdon directed to go motor racing (something that it had to learn from scratch) but it also had to compete head on with the Cooper Car Co team, which was reborn as Cooper-Britax-Downton.

Throughout 1969 John Rhodes and John Handley (Abingdon) fought head-to-head against C-B-D (Gordon Spice and Steve Neal) and against the Broadspeed Escorts. Honours were split between the teams, with the most successful driver (Spice)

finishing second in the 1.3-litre class. It took Abingdon until late summer to make up for a total lack of previous experience but it all came right at the Austrian Salzburgring in October, when Rhodes and Handley took first and second overall in a tightly contested 1.3-litre race.

Amazingly, while all this brotherly fighting was going on, a private team, Equipe Arden, built up a new eight-port 970S, which produced phenomenal horsepower. Alec Poole concentrated on the British Championship, completely obliterated his opposition, and won the series outright.

Above: Although the entire time it drove its heart out, the Mini-Cooper could not quite beat the 200bhp Porsche 911s in the 1968 Monte Carlo Rally. This 1275S was driven by Tony Fall into fourth place.

Right: In 1969 Alec Poole drove this incredibly highly tuned Mini-Cooper 970S to win his category of the British Saloon Car Championship. Because the Championship ran to a class-improvement marking system, he also won the series outright.

Handley's experience allied to British Vita's preparation skills saw this friendly little team win its class and, due to the marking system, also win the European Championship outright. For the Cooper Car Co, however, it was more of an uphill struggle. Even though they were now equipped with fuel-injected 1,293cc engines, which produced about 130bhp, Rhodes and Neal had to fight a running battle with Broadspeed's 145bhp Escort GTs. If the Fords had been more reliable, the battle would have been even tougher but the good news for Abingdon was that John Rhodes once again won the 1.3-litre Championship class and finished third overall in the series.

Modernising the Mini: ADO20 takes over

Just before the end of 1969, British Leyland was finally ready to launch a major package of Mini improvements. To make sure that these were not submerged by the interest that was otherwise going to be centred on the also-new Mini Clubman/1275GT types (described in the next chapter), this introduction was held back until November, after the London Motor Show had closed its doors.

Ever since Leyland's top managers had walked into Longbridge in the spring of 1968, they had been determined to stamp their authority on 'their' new business. At a stroke, what had once been the BMC business was rechristened Austin-Morris, with ex-Triumph man George Turnbull drafted in as the new Managing Director.

The autocratic management methods of Alec Issigonis – and the Great Man himself – were speedily replaced by Technical Director Harry Webster, who had made such a name for himself at Triumph in the 1960s.

Once Leyland's accountants had examined the Austin-Morris finances, they concluded that although one in every two cars being produced at Longbridge and Cowley was a Mini, it was not making much profit for the corporation. Accordingly, Leyland set out to get to grips with the Mini phenomenon and make some real money out of it.

Rationalisation, not diversification, it decided, was the key to this. It was not alone, for this had not escaped the 'old'

management: even while the British Leyland takeover/merger was going ahead in January 1968, Mini assembly at Cowley was closing down, to make way for the Austin Maxi. Henceforth, and for the next 32 years, all UK Mini assembly would take place at Longbridge: sales and production continued to surge ahead, with the two millionth example being built in May 1969.

To make coherent sense of the way in which the Mini range was developing, the planners decided on a twin-pronged course of action: to introduce an upmarket evolution of the type (this would be the Clubman/1275GT) and (within financial limits) to update the existing models as thoroughly as possible.

In BMC-speak this was the point at which ADO15 (the original Mini) became ADO20 (a revised version), which was changed in so many ways. Not only was this the moment at which all 'badges' were abandoned but when reversion was made to 'dry' suspension and when wind-up windows were included in the entry-level Mini specification for the very first time. As already noted, the Countryman/ Traveller option was to be dropped (in future it would only figure on the Clubman derivative).

Compared with the MkII of 1967–1969, although the style was virtually the same, in fact much of the bodyshell had been changed. Not only was there a revised floorpan, boot floor, and windscreen surround but the external door hinges had now been abandoned in favour of the concealed hinges which had already been fitted to the Elf/Hornet/Mini Clubman derivatives.

The doors themselves were now fitted with wind-up windows of the Elf/Hornet type (which were not the same as those fitted to Australian-assembled Minis), which were a real advance – except that it meant that the doors were considerably thicker and that there was no space for those much-loved bins.

Mechanically, the major change was a reversion from Hydrolastic ('wet') to rubber cone ('dry') suspension, which effectively wound the clock back five years. This was done for three main reasons: one (but only until 1971) being to delineate this Mini from the larger Mini Clubman, another being to reduce product costs, and the third to meet customer preferences.

'Wet' or 'dry'? Although Hydrolastic ('wet') suspension had built itself a satisfactory service record (and let's not forget that it was also standard on the 1100/1300, Maxi, and 1800 models), there was no doubt that some customers did not like the quality of the ride which was on offer. In spite of what gung-ho motoring writers usually

had to say, British Leyland's marketing staffs had concluded that a perceived, minor, reduction in ride comfort would be acceptable on this entry-level car. And so it was – Hydrolastic suspension was never again seen on this type of Mini.

Other mechanical changes/updates included a change to negative-earth electrics (this was just one instance of a change that was gradually taking place across the British motor industry at this time). Four-wheel drum brakes and cross-ply tyres were still standard on these cars and, as before, the 850-engined types had the long gear lever, those with 998cc having the Mini-Cooper type of remote control change.

Mini becomes a marque

From this point, all such cars were Minis – not Austins and not Morrises but Minis – so no matter which showroom one patronised, the cars were totally identical. Henceforth there was just one range of badges, grilles, and colour schemes and all cars were fitted with the corporate British Leyland roundel on the front wings, immediately behind the front wheelarch openings.

This is how the new range lined up:

Mini 850   £596, plus £14 for the heater. Replaced the Mini MkII

Mini 1000   £675, plus £14 for the heater. Replaced the Mini MkII Super

Automatic transmission cost an extra £98

For 1970, therefore, there would be a total of six 'unbadged' cars in the Mini range: 850, 1000, Clubman, Clubman Estate, 1275GT, and Cooper S. Because the Clubman/1275GT was such a major departure from the previous Mini mainstream and represents a major kick-start to British Leyland's development philosophy for these cars, I have described it in the next chapter.

In the meantime, sales and production of the entire Mini range continued to surge ahead. Even though Longbridge was regularly hit by unofficial strike action (which brought assembly to a halt for considerable periods), Mini output moved up from 278,950 in 1970, to 318,475 in 1971 (an all-time record), and to 306,937 in 1972.

Below: To British Leyland in 1969, this was ADO20 but to Mini enthusiasts this was the first UK-built version of the original-shape car to carry 'Mini' (instead of other marque) badges and to have wind-up windows.

1969–1990
City, Mayfair, Clubman, 1275GT, and special editions

As already described in the previous chapter, in the autumn of 1969 British Leyland substantially revised the existing Mini – in business-speak terms by turning ADO15 into ADO20 – but in parallel with this it also introduced the first-ever substantially reshaped Mini. At the same time as ADO20 was taking over, British Leyland also introduced the longer/square-nosed Mini Clubman range. Although the two cars were revealed several weeks apart, the new structural engineering involved was so intermingled that they were phased in together, at Longbridge.

There is a fascinating sub-plot to this development. Not only must I relate all the facts about the Clubman and 1275GT models but I should also analyse the rationale behind their introduction. Why, for instance, did British Leyland have to drop the Mini-Cooper to make way for the 1275GT – and what was the long nose all about? Was there a hidden agenda here? Were further changes planned but later cancelled?

Unpopular changes

The new Minis caused controversy at the time – and still do. It was British Leyland, not BMC, which introduced these long-nose Minis and purists received them with a storm of protest. The problem, at the time, was that British Leyland was seen as a murderer. Not only had it introduced a car that looked different from the original but had immediately killed off the Mini-Cooper (but not the Cooper S) to make way for it.

At first it seemed as if British Leyland just couldn't win. It wasn't that these were poor Minis – if you look at the specifications, you'll see that in some ways they were better than before – but they arrived at exactly the wrong time, when British Leyland's reputation was already starting to wobble and the media was ready to criticise almost anything new.

Then, and later, nothing which the cars could do ever erased that initial impression. Even though nearly 400,000 were sold before the Mini Metro arrived in 1980 (and replaced the Clubman/1275GT models), they never really recovered from those initial criticisms. But was it all bad news? If you put away your prejudices, what should you then think?

Left: The long-nose Mini Clubman appeared at the end of 1969, and caused controversy because of its style, but immediately began to sell very well. Before it was discontinued in 1980, nearly half a million saloons and estate cars were produced.

Long-nose reasoning

Let's get one thing clear right now. The Clubman was definitely conceived by BMC in 1967 before British Leyland was formed, though we know that Sir Donald Stokes of Leyland inspired the birth of the 1275GT. You only have to know a little about the time it took BMC/British Leyland to make new body press tools in the 1960s to realise this: it was not thought possible to commission a new style – from clay model to showroom examples – in less than two years.

In 1967, with the future and new crash-test legislation in mind, BMC not only wanted to re-engineer the Mini but at the same time to provide more engine bay space. First thoughts came from stylist/packaging engineer/product planner Roy Haynes, who had joined BMC from Ford. Haynes was based at Cowley, not

Longbridge, and was directly responsible to Managing Director Joe Edwards – he had no responsibility to Alec Issigonis.

With Sir Leonard Lord now retired and Sir George Harriman more open to discussion and persuasion, the dynamic Edwards's great wish was to sort out the mishmash that was the Mini range. Not only did he want to prepare the Mini for the 1970s but he wanted to produce a derivative that would move the range upmarket, take over from the Riley Elf/Wolseley Hornet models, and abandon separate Austin and Morris badges, in order to reduce the number of 'nearly-the-same' versions.

Alec Issigonis's space-saving philosophy had already been partly abandoned, for this was no longer a Mini in which the body skin panels were wrapped around the

running gear just as closely as possible. There was, apparently, the possibility that larger/different engines than the ubiquitous A-series might be fitted later but in the event these never actually reached production. There was space, too, for a front-mounted radiator, which would have been a great improvement; although I often saw prototypes running around at Longbridge, these did not make it into production – until 1996!

Later in 1968, on the other hand (and a full year before the longer-nose car made its bow), British Leyland added a 1275GT model to that plan, not only to start rationalising its A-series engine range (and to reduce costs!) but to start phasing out the Cooper name badge. By this time, as is readily apparent, Alec Issigonis's influence on future Mini policy and on new products

Opposite: A new look for 1970, squared-up rather than rounded. The Clubman/1275GT style was controversial, but sold well.

in general was on the wane, while that shadowy profession, product planning, was becoming important.

Motor industry analyst Rob Golding told us more: 'American Filmer Paradise, the sales director of the day, wanted the car to have a more upmarket appeal in order to lift the prices, and the man who met the brief was [stylist] Roy Haynes, who had been recruited from Ford. Throughout the late 1960s, Haynes was being pushed by Managing Director Joe Edwards to come up with a completely new body for the Mini.

The drawings that emerged were no great improvement and plans to relaunch the car were shelved. The halfway house of the Clubman front was adopted instead...It did increase the usefulness of the under-bonnet space a little but increased the drag of the car and the fuel consumption.'

It was, in other words, a classic marketing move – to drive down the costs while putting up prices. BMC, it seems, had realised it was not making money out of the Mini and thought it was time for a change!

Below: When viewed from the tail, there was virtually nothing to distinguish a Clubman/1275GT from the existing AD020 model – but look closely and the badge gives the game away.

All change for 1970

When the three new Mini-based cars – Clubman, Clubman Estate, and 1275GT – appeared in October 1969, they introduced the first major package of changes for the Mini. Not only was there a new style but much equipment was added – and the individual badges finally disappeared. As already described, henceforth a Mini would be badged as a Mini – not as an Austin, Morris, Riley, Wolseley or whatever – which was bowing to reality, for this is what you and I had been doing for years anyway! From that moment, the Austin and Morris badges would only be found in the spares parts bins. However, that wasn't the final end of this story – for de-badged, stand-alone, Minis would officially become Rover Minis in the 1990s...

Many of the changes described below were shared with the short-nose/ADO20-type of Mini shell too. For use in the Clubman/1275GT cars, the squared-up, long-nose, body style wasn't the only change made to the Mini's body. At the same time, the external door hinges were dropped in favour of conventional-type concealed hinges and the wind-up windows that had already been seen in the Riley Elf and Wolseley Hornet were also standardised. The 1275GTs not only got appropriate badging but were also decorated with a pair of then-fashionable 'speed stripes' on each flank, just above the doors.

Inside the cabin, there was a new facia/instrument layout, with two dials in the Clubman (three dials for the 1275GT) positioned ahead of the driver's eyes, face level 'eyeball' vents to provide improved ventilation, and a new-style steering wheel. According to publicity claims, the seats and driving position had been improved but for the passengers it wasn't always easy to see where or how, for the steering column was still located in the usual sit-up-and-beg position. The bad news, too, was that, to make space for the wind-down windows, there was no longer any space for bins in the doors and across-the-car elbow-room was less than it had been on the original Minis.

This 1978-model 1275GT looks very smart and, apart from the wheels (which were factory optional extras) is just as it was when it left Longbridge nearly 30 years before this photograph was taken.

Below: Neat and integrated styling of the Clubman/1275GT nose included sculpted front bumpers and sidelamp/turn indicators hidden away underneath.

Below right:In the 1970s there was a fashion for 'speed stripes', which several manufacturers, including British Leyland, adopted. Such stripes were fitted to the 1275GT throughout its 11-year life.

Under the skin, the 'chassis' was familiar and like that of 1967–1969 Minis, for both the saloons had Hydrolastic suspension, the familiar pushrod A-series engines, and four-speed all-synchromesh gearbox-in-sump transmissions. The four-speed AP automatic transmission was optional on the Clubman but never on the 1275GT.

(Incidentally, in October and November 1969 British Leyland's hapless PR department repeatedly got its facts thoroughly confused – but there was nothing strange about that, as it happened regularly at this stage. At launch time it stated that there would be a 1275GT automatic, weeks later the company then changed its mind, then dithered in the face of magazine criticism, and only decided that the automatic box would not be

Right: All Clubman/1275GT types had swivelling 'eyeball' face-level air vents at the sides of the facia, this being a big advance over the original Mini 'fug-stirring' installation.

Far right: By the late 1970s, Mini facia layouts, like this from the 1275GT, had come a long way from the very stark and original variety. The 1970s-type Clubman models had twin dials, the 1275GT having three-dials. The two-spoke steering wheel was introduced in 1976.

Right: Neat and unobtrusive packaging/styling of 'door furniture' in the 1275GT – a far cry from the Issigonis pull-string arrangement of the original cars.

Left: Like the original Mini, the Clubman/1275GT had a very restricted space for pedals and feet. Alec Issigonis's insistence on making the car tiny meant that the front wheel wells pushed the pedals across towards the centreline of the car.

available six weeks later. That's why the media was so scathing about British Leyland at the time...)

In its original form, the Clubman was mechanically very similar to the short-nose 998cc Mini. Naturally, there was also an estate car version, which melded the new long nose and wind-up-window doors with the existing Traveller/Countryman cabin, replacing the original Traveller and Countryman types, which were discontinued at that point.

Left: First introduced on the 1275GT of 1969, this three-dial instrument cluster would later be adopted on other Mini models. This was the second type of steering wheel used on these 1275GT models and replaced the original three-spoke variety.

The 1275GT, on the other hand, was a new mechanical mix. On the one hand, this was the first Mini to use a single-SU 1,275cc A-series engine. This was rated at 59bhp, which made it nearly identical with the bigger-bodied Austin and Morris 1300 models. Although it was more powerful than the 998cc Mini-Cooper, it was much less powerful than the Mini-Cooper 1275S (which continued), though British Leyland hoped that the use of a 3.65:1 final drive ratio (instead of the 3.44:1 of the Cooper 1275S) would help. Like the Mini-Cooper S, the 1275GT had Hydrolastic suspension, 7½in front disc brakes, 145-10in radial-ply tyres on 4½in rims – and a brake servo was standard.

Above: Now you see it, now you don't...In this shot of a 1978 1275GT, the water-shield over the distributor and high-tension leads is fitted while...

Above: ...here the shield has been removed so that we can show off the late-1970s engine bay, which now included an alternator instead of a dynamo.

Left: The Clubman/1275GT models shared the same 80in-wheelbase platform, and two-door cabin, as other Mini saloons.

103

The Mini range for 1970

With deliveries of both Clubman and 1275GT models starting in late 1969, alongside the ADO20-style Mini, British Leyland thought it had a nicely integrated range, which lined up like this:

Model	Engine size	Basic price	Total price with tax
Mini 850 MkII	848cc	£455	£596 6s 5d
Mini 1000 MkII	998cc	£515	£674 13s 1d
Clubman	998cc	£550	£720 6s 11d
Clubman Estate	998cc	£583	£763 8s 7d
Automatic extra (on above)	–	£75	£97 18s 4d
1275GT	1,275cc	£637	£833 18s 7d
Mini-Cooper S	1,275cc	£720	£941 12s 9d

Above right: Old tail, new nose – but the Clubman estate car was very popular. Nearly 200,000 were sold between 1969 and 1980.

Right: Combining the original Mini Traveller shell with the Clubman nose, and decorating the sides with a broad false-wood stripe, produced a very successful version of the latest range in 1970.

Opposite: Exploded in every possible way! This display layout shows the design elements of the 1275GT, as launched in 1969.

Rising sales

In fairness to British Leyland, it must have got the product planning right at this stage, for in the next few years total Mini sales rose persistently to record levels. In 1968 246,066 Minis had been built, rising to 254,957 in 1969, 278,950 in 1970, and to a record 318,475 in 1971. Of these totals, about 40,000 Clubman/1275GT models were being built every year, not perhaps as many as originally hoped but still ample to justify the investment in new front-end body tooling.

An 11-year career

Cars of this Clubman/1275GT shape would then stay in production until the summer of 1980, when they finally made way for the new Austin Mini Metro (which, in spite of picking up the legendary Mini name and sharing the same basic engine/transmission layout, had a totally different, larger platform and body style). Although the last cars were recognisably the same as the original cars built in 1969, many small changes – styling, equipment, and mechanical – were made along the way.

Mechanically, the most important change on Clubman/1275GT types was to revert from Hydrolastic to rubber cone suspension in mid-1971 (this change, of course, had been made to 'short-nose' Minis when they were de-badged in 1969). To

Right: Smart, optional, 12in alloy wheels on this 1275GT of the late 1970s. By this period in the Mini's history, British Leyland's marketing staff had moved a long way from the stark, simple, no-extras philosophy of the original Issigonis Mini.

Far right: As the years progressed, Mini packaging became ever more crowded. On this 1275GT, with the 12in wheels fitted from 1974, the discs have grown and the brake calipers are larger than before.

follow up, the 1275GT was then given 12in diameter wheels and larger front disc brakes (but without a servo – another method of cost cutting) in 1974, while run-flat Dunlop Denovo tyres were standardised on the 1275GT in August 1977.

To upgrade the Clubman even further, for the 1976 model-year manual-transmission cars gained a 45bhp/1,098cc engine. All types were equipped with an alternator at the end of 1972, Clubman models got radial-ply tyres as standard

soon afterwards, while plunging-type constant velocity driveshaft joints were fitted from June 1973.

As with many other British Leyland cars of the period, there was a stream of trim and equipment improvements – this, incidentally, making it more difficult for modern Clubman and 1275GT owners to restore their cars to the correct period specification! For instance:

June 1974 Heated rear window standardised
October 1975 Reclining front seats and cloth trim standardised.
May 1976 New-style black grille, new column-mounted control stalks, along with new rocker-style switchgear, larger pedals, moulded carpets, and a different steering column lock. The 1275GT also got a new seat style and extra interior equipment.
July 1977 New wheel trims, leather steering wheel, tinted glass, and reversing lamps were all standardised.

One thing, though, never changed. Like every other Mini, these cars steered, handled, and behaved like no other car in the world. The Clubman might have been a few inches longer, and slightly heavier, than the short-nose Minis but that never seemed to affect the car's response.

Maybe the 1275GT could have used a lot more power (after the Mini-Cooper S was dropped in June 1971 it was much the most powerful derivative in the range) but British Leyland always protested that it was offering 90mph performance at a much lower price than it could ever have sold a Mini-Cooper S.

In other words, it was good but not sensational and, because it didn't have a regular 'works' competition record, some enthusiasts couldn't warm to it. But you can't argue with the sales figures...

Alec Issigonis, no doubt, would not have approved, for he did not like styling, as such. The Clubman/1275GT nose was more square, and less rounded, than the original Mini of 1975.

When the long-nose Clubman/1275GT model was announced in 1969, its looks caused a great deal of controversy. In the end, though, British Leyland would sell nearly 600,000 of all types, saloons and estates.

Left: As with the original Minis, the late-1970s models retained their drop-down boot lid, though the number plate was no longer hinged. On this particular car, there is a neatly placed radio aerial, above and ahead of the right-side tail lamp.

Right: This seat cover style was so typical of many British Leyland cars of the mid- and late 1970s, including the Austin Allegro, the MGB, and the Triumph TR7.

Left: This 1275GT has the later, enlarged, fuel tank, while the owner has preserved the original very simple toolkit. As ever, the boot lid let down from the bottom hinges, to increase potential carrying volume.

The last of the 1275 Cooper S

As I have already noted, the last of the 1,275cc-engined MkII Mini-Cooper S types was built in 1969/1970 but the ADO20-based MkIII did not appear until March 1970. This, of course, was the only early-type Mini-Cooper S ever to have the ADO20/wind-up-window style of bodywork and should never be confused with the reborn Mini-Cooper/Mini-Cooper S models, which would appear 20 years later!

For the first and only time, here was a Mini-Cooper to share the same grille as other Minis of the day but enthusiasts could still pick out the special nature of this car, by its twin fuel tanks, its badging, its wide-bore exhaust pipe, and, of course, by its performance. Like earlier MkII types, an engine oil cooler was hidden away under the bonnet.

Two product-planning quirks, which British Leyland never bothered to explain, were the lack of duotone paintwork – all MkIIIs wore roof colours that matched the rest of the car – and the retention of Hydrolastic suspension. This last feature was odd, not only because every other short-nose Mini had already reverted to 'dry' rubber-cone suspension but because it was previous Cooper S customers who had complained most strongly about the feel of Hydrolastic suspension in the first place!

The only important development change made to this model was that from October 1970 a black moulded ignition-wiring shield was fitted under the bonnet and at the same time an ignition/steering lock was standardised.

Although this type was only in production from March 1970 until June 1971, no fewer than 19,511 cars were built in that time. Mind you, one might not have seen many of them on a casual visit to Longbridge, as the vast majority (around 18,000) of them were sent as CKD kits for assembly in overseas plants.

When the very last Mini-Cooper 1275S was produced at Longbridge in mid-1971, this brought to an end a decade in which Cooper-badged cars had raised the profile of the entire Mini range. As far as the enthusiast was concerned, this was a real tragedy and it also meant that this was no longer a nice little earner for John Cooper.

Lord Stokes, on the other hand, was satisfied about the whole business, smugly confident that the less-excitingly specified 1275GT would take over. In sales terms, perhaps he was right – 110,673 1275GTs would be built in a decade – but in image terms he was quite wrong. Nearly 20 years later, British Leyland's successor company, the Rover Group, reintroduced a Cooper-badged car – that story will be told in the next chapter.

Soon after the MkIII Cooper S had gone on sale, incidentally, British Leyland celebrated the building of the millionth Mini to go to an export market. On 21 April, Managing Director George Turnbull handed over a car to Gunnar Elk of British Leyland Norway. At that point, too, the statistics churned out, telling us that no fewer than 190,000 Minis (built up, or in kits for Innocenti to complete) had already gone to Italy, which was the largest export market, and 176,000 to Australia.

Left: Mini racing was extremely competitive at all times – especially for this 1275GT, which was nudged into a spin and roll at one point. The car was badly damaged but the driver came to no harm.

1970: The last 'works' Minis in rallying

Before the motor sport department at Abingdon was abruptly closed down in the autumn of 1970, there was time for a handful of Mini-Cooper entries to be made. Because the department was completely bound up with the preparation of cars for the monumental 16,000-mile *Daily Mirror* World Cup Rally, these did not even begin until April.

First of all, for the World Cup Rally, Abingdon prepared a highly tuned and very non-standard 1275GT. No one thought that a Mini could survive such a six-week test, so the intention was for the Handley/Easter car to be a 'hare' and to take a few headlines before it expired. The breakdown duly came in the first few days, when the highly tuned engine suffered from fuel supply problems and blew a piston.

Weeks later, and re-prepared to run in 'prototype' form in the Scottish rally,

Paddy Hopkirk urged the same 1275GT into second place overall, this actually being the last ever finish to be recorded by a 'works' Mini of any type.

The axe fell later in the year and the last 'works' Mini of all – a 1275S driven by Brian Culcheth, started the Australian Rally of the Hills in November 1970 and finished fourth overall. Thereafter, it was private owners who carried on using Minis for some years, both in rallies and on the circuits.

Mini in the 1970s

For the next decade the ADO20-style Mini, wind-up windows and all, sold steadily and still in great numbers. Inevitably, the longer-nose Clubman/1275GT took away many sales from the snub-nose car but overall figures held up very well. Even by 1980, when the public, in truth, must have been getting bored with seeing the same specification/same style Minis in the showrooms, no fewer than 150,067 were still built.

Why was the Mini never substantially changed during the 1970s? Not, for sure, because there was no desire to do so but because British Leyland could always find other destinations for its investment capital and invent other priorities. From an accountant's angle, this was probably justified, for sales did not dip below 200,000 a year until 1978.

(Where did the investment go instead? Into major new models like the Morris Marina in 1971, the Austin Allegro in 1973, the ADO71 Princess in 1975, and into engines like the six-cylinder E6 of 1972 and the O-series of 1978. Much money, too, was spent preparing for the Mini Metro but that would not become obvious until 1980.)

In any case, although 9X (a proposed replacement) was never seen again and Alec Issigonis was sidelined (to become the Director of Research and Development – effectively a non-job, created to keep him out of mischief), behind the scenes British Leyland engineers made other repeated attempts during the 1970s to 'replace' the Mini, by proposing major alterations and improvements. Wider cars, reskinned cars, re-engined cars, restyled cars – all on the same 80in wheelbase platform with 'dry'

Above: Serious stuff – the most powerful of all Mini engines were the 1.3-litre units fitted with cross-flow eight-port cylinder heads and fuel injection. This was the four-wheel-drive rallycross car of the early 1970s.

Right: Have you ever seen a Mini with a rear axle before? Thought not – this being the installation of the unique four-wheel-drive rallycross car, which Special Tuning built at Abingdon in the early 1970s.

suspension – and even a completely new project (ADO 74) were proposed but all fell by the wayside. Even the ADO 88 project, which once looked set fair to become the replacement, grew persistently larger during design and development, was eventually reskinned and renamed LC8 and appeared in 1980 as the Austin Mini Metro, alongside the Mini and not able to replace it.

Through and around all this, not only did British Leyland bring forward a series of improvement packages for the ADO20 models but it also began producing a series of Mini 'special editions'. Because special editions were invariably based on an existing model, I have grouped the first of these towards the end of this chapter.

In the meantime, Mini 850 and 1000 saloons continued throughout the 1970s, along with Mini vans and pick-ups. The light commercial vehicles tended to pick up the same improvements as those applied to the 850 saloon. The following summarises the important updates to standard equipment:

1970/1971 Steering lock on some models, later standardised to meet legislation.
Late 1972 A remote-control gear change was finally specified on 850s as well as 1000s. This was the point at which a rod-operated change (as opposed to one with a long cast alloy extension) was fitted, along with an electrical alternator.
February 1973 Radial-ply tyres.
Spring 1974 Front-seat inertia-reel safety belts (previously optional) and, finally, a fresh-air heater.
May 1976 A revised steering column, with twin control stalks, plus revised switch panel, pedals, moulded carpets, and revised suspension settings. Face-level ventilation standard on Mini 1000.
July 1977 Matt black grille, padded steering wheel. On 1000 only, rake-adjustable front seats, enhanced trim.
July 1979 Two 850 models – Mini City and Mini 850 Super de Luxe – replaced the Mini 850, with different trim levels, Super de Luxe had the three-dial instrument panel and face-level ventilation.
Early 1980 7½-gallon single fuel tank replaced the old 5½-gallon type.

Mini in the 1980s

After the Austin Mini-Metro appeared at the end of 1980, with Vanden Plas and MG derivatives following up from 1982, it was clear that the classic Mini would have to go on marking time for some years to come. Production fell from 150,067 in 1980 to 49,956 in 1983 and to a mere 33,720 in 1986. For Austin-Rover, as the group was currently calling itself, there must have been a moment of pride and relief when the five millionth car was produced in 1986, with TV personality Noel Edmonds providing the glamour behind that photo-opportunity.

Once again, this was a decade in which the Mini was starved of investment, for new models such as the Triumph Acclaim, Austin Maestro, Austin Montego, Rover 800, and Rover 200 all took precedence.

What became known as the Rover Group took the view that as long as there was a demand for the Mini, and as long as the necessary engineering changes could be made to keep the car legally in the marketplace, then it would continue to be on sale. Even so, there were more genuine technical updates – 12in wheels and front-wheel disc brakes, for instance – than in the 1970s.

During the 1980s, however, the range of different Minis contracted markedly. Once the Metro had appeared at the end of 1980, the long-nose Clubman and 1275GT models disappeared at once, which meant that the practical little Clubman Estate was also discontinued, though it carried on in Mini 1000 HL guise until 1982. Mini vans and pick-ups stuttered on until May 1983, after which they, too, were dropped. From that point, therefore, the only Minis being made had two-door saloon bodyshells.

This is how the Mini's 1980s career evolved:

August 1980 Mini City and Mini 850 Super de Luxe assembly ended. Henceforth the vans and pick-ups were the only Minis still using 848cc engines.
October 1980 The revised model range of 998cc Minis was the entry-level City, the 1000, and the new 1000HL saloon and estate, which had a Clubman-type interior, including the two-dial instrument pod.

April 1982 City rebadged as City E, with higher (2.95:1) final drive ratio and high-compression engine. 1000HL became 1000HLE and gained similar mechanical improvements. Cars now distinguished by black bumpers.
The last of the estate car derivatives – called 1000HLE in the final months – were produced in the summer of 1982.
September 1982 1000HLE displaced by mechanically similar Mayfair (this revived a 1930s-style Austin model name), now the luxury model in the range, with upmarket trim and furnishings such as velour upholstery, cut-pile carpets, tinted glass, front seat head restraints, and a radio as standard. Sir Alec Issigonis, it is thought, did not like the way that the Mini's character was changing.

Above: When the five millionth Mini was ready to be built in 1986, British Leyland hired Noel Edmonds to give it a good send-off.

May 1983 Vans and pick-ups were finally discontinued. After this, the only Minis in production were two-door saloons. October 1984 All surviving Minis gained 12in road wheels with 145SR-12in radial-ply tyres, plus front-wheel disc brakes, along with black plastic wheelarch extension mouldings.

November 1985 City E trim/fittings upgraded, with twin-instrument pack, face-level ventilation, four-spoke (Metro-type) steering wheel. Mayfair given three-instrument pack (including rev counter), new three-spoke wheel, and upgraded trim/carpets.

October 1986 Rear seat lap safety belts standardised.

June 1987 Austin badges finally deleted.

August 1988 City E renamed City, now with three-spoke steering wheel and front-seat headrests. Mayfair now with stereo radio/cassette installation as standard, trim enhancements, and slightly upgraded engine. A brake vacuum servo was standardised two months later.

June 1989 An exhaust catalytic converter became optional.

More development changes would be introduced in the 1990s, though the main news in that, the final decade, was the relaunch of the Mini-Cooper brand and a major update of the model, which belatedly followed in 1996.

Special editions of the 1970s and 1980s

Somewhere in America – it had to be America, right? – someone invented that famous advertising saying: 'Don't sell the sausage – sell the sizzle!'. This, in essence, is what all special-edition – sometimes advertised as 'limited edition' – cars are all about. It's one way of making a thoroughly familiar car look, and feel, a bit more special – it usually works wonders for showroom demand.

It's fair to say that most special editions were conceived to keep the showrooms busy when things were otherwise a little quiet and it's also fair to say that they were rarely faster, merely prettier, than the standard models on which they were based. At the time, though, and sometimes for many years after that, they were looked on as rather special.

Who was the very first manufacturer to invent this tactic? Probably an American, although the origins are lost in the mists of time, but the first-ever British 'special edition' was probably the Morris Minor 1,000,000 – of which 350 lilac-hued examples were built in 1961.

With Minis selling at more than 200,000–250,000 cars a year until the mid-1970s, neither BMC nor British Leyland needed to create any specials for a long time. Then, as the Mini gradually began to show its age, the first limited-number types began to appear.

After 1976, when the first-ever UK-market Mini-special – the Limited Edition – appeared, the pace quickened. After 1983, every year saw yet another special version appearing in the showrooms – there being three different types in each of 1989 and 1990. Some models commemorated an important Mini anniversary – the last of the period being the Mini Thirty of 1989, which naturally came along 30 years after the birth of the original car.

When a carmaker like British Leyland, Austin-Rover, or Rover produces a special edition, the ground rules are that special editions look much more different than they actually are. Under the skin there would always be a familiar model but visually it would have a substantial makeover.

In every case, the company's special-edition Minis were always based on the familiar short-nose ADO20 two-door saloon. There were no special Clubman-based cars and no special estates – so if anyone ever offers you one, don't believe him/her. They did not exist!

There were many good reasons, incidentally, why the company rarely altered the mechanical specification or uprated the running gear. A generation ago that might have been feasible but by the 1970s and 1980s there were so many new legislative requirements and Type Approval rules to be met that it simply made no economic sense.

Special edition Minis: dates and features

Each of these special edition types was based on the same 10ft long four-seater saloon, complete with rubber cone suspension and radial-ply tyres. All cars had 998cc engines unless otherwise stated. Except that I have not mentioned special/distinctive badging and details such as extra mirrors, badges, and decals, this is what each type had to offer over the then-standard Mini (and the model on which it was based). In many cases one feature or fitting was used for the very first time on a Mini (but was maybe adopted later as a 'mainstream' fitment). In that case, I have listed it here under Innovations.

This is a complete list of UK-market special-edition Minis produced from 1976 to 1990, with their 'base model' and their distinguishing features:

1976 Limited Edition 1000 (Based on the 1000): Green and white paint, MGB-style striped brushed-nylon seats. Priced at £1,406 with 3,000 made. Innovations: Face-level ventilation and reclining seats.

1979 1100 Special (1000): Silver or Rose paintwork, tartan check seat covers, many extra touches. Innovations: 1,098cc/45bhp engine, the first and only time used in a short-nose Mini. Cast alloy wheels. Black wheelarch extensions (as original sold by

Special Tuning, from Abingdon, for motor sport purposes). 1275GT-style three-dial instrument binnacle. Priced at £3,300 with 5,100 produced.

1983 Sprite (City): Using the old Austin-Healey model name, in Cinnabar Red or Primula Yellow. Innovations: New (pre-Mayfair) three-instrument-dial binnacle, four-spoke steering wheel. Cost £3,334 with 2,500 produced.

1984 25 (Mayfair): Silver paintwork, velvet trim, leather-trimmed three-spoke steering wheel. Cost £3,865 with 5,000 produced. Innovations: 1275GT-type 12in wheels, front-wheel disc brakes, tinted glass, radio/cassette as standard.

City of Westminster
CARNABY ST.
W.1
MARY QUANT
COLOUR SHOP
MARY QUANT
COLOUR SHOP
Designer
E477LJD

standard and with a Targa Red paint job/red spats. Priced at £3,898 with 1,500 UK examples built.

Piccadilly (City E): Like the Ritz and Chelsea but in Cashmere Gold with wheelarch extensions and spats and plastic wheel trims over steel wheels (instead of alloy wheels). Cost £3,928 with 2,500 produced.

1987 Park Lane (City E): Like Ritz/Chelsea/Piccadilly but with all-black paint job, wheelarch extensions, tinted windows, and striped seat interior. Priced at £4,194 with 4,000 produced (1,500 for UK sale).

Advantage (City E): With a Wimbledon/tennis theme, all-white paint job, black wheelarch extensions, and 'Advantage' script on the doors. Priced at £4,286 with 4,675 produced (2,500 sold in UK).

1988 Red Hot/Jet Black (City): Red or black paintwork, respectively, with black wheelarch extensions, and tinted glass in each case. Cost £4,382 with 2,000 for UK sale, plus 4,000 for export.

Designer (City): Available in Black or Diamond White, with grey wheelarch extensions, special interior, leather-bound

steering wheel. Priced at £4,654 with 2,000 produced. Innovations: Black and white vertical striped seats.

1989 Racing/Flame/Rose/Sky (City): British Racing Green/white roof, red/white roof, white/pink roof, or white/blue roof respectively, all with black wheelarch extensions. Sports steering wheel and rev counter on first two types, otherwise all types nearly identical. Priced at £4,795, £4,795, £4,695, and £4,695 respectively. Numbers built: Flame/Racing 2,000, Sky and Rose 1,000 in total.

Thirty (Mayfair): Cherry Red or black, luxurious trim, with wheelarch extensions. Cost £5,599 for manual transmission cars with 2,800 for sale in the UK, plus 200 with optional automatic transmission. Innovations: Minilite-style alloy wheels (pre-Mini-Cooper). This was also the very first special edition Mini to have an automatic transmission option.

This was not the end of the special edition story, for many more such cars would follow in the 1990s. These are listed and described in the later chapters.

So, if you are in the market for a special edition Mini, you have a problem – making a choice – for there was a multitude of different models. Even so, they were relatively rare. Although around 55,000 'specials' may have been sold in Britain over the years, that equates to only one in every 100 'mainstream' Minis produced. This explains why 'classic' special-edition types still sell at a slight premium and why a few Registers have sprung up to service them.

For today's Mini enthusiasts, the problem is not of supply but of upkeep. When the time comes for restoration and repairs, it should always be possible to match paint colours and most of the exterior fittings but there will usually be a major difficulty in finding the correct seat materials, trim panels, decals, and badges.

Red, blue, and grey velvet material to restore Ritz seats? Little green tennis ball badges on Advantage seats? Mary Quant 'Daisy' logos on 1988 Designers? The list goes on but the hunt may be worth it – in each and every case, Rover only built a limited number of those cars.

Above: The 1985 Ritz special edition was based on the City E with special paintwork, wheels, and interior trim.

1985 Ritz (City E): Silver leaf paint job, silver wheelarch extensions, red/blue/grey striped seats, reclining fronts. Cost £3,798 with 3,725 produced (2,000 for the UK). Innovations: Standard 12in Mayfair-style wheels, which were still optional extras on the 'base' car.

1986 Chelsea (City E): Built at the same time as the five-millionth Mini. Similar to the Ritz, with a rev counter as

Right: The Mini Thirty was the first special edition with optional automatic transmission. The distinctive Minilite-style wheels were used on a production Mini for the first time.

Specifications: Mini Clubman

ENGINE

Description

In-line four-cylinder with cast iron block and cylinder head. Chain-driven camshaft in block, pushrod-operated overhead valves. Heart-shaped combustion chambers. Aluminium alloy pistons, forged steel connecting rods. Three-bearing counter-weighted crankshaft

Capacity

998cc (60.9cu in), 1,098cc (67.0cu in)

Bore and stroke

998cc 64.59mm x 76.2mm (2.54in x 3.00in)
1,098cc 64.59mm x 83.73mm (2.54in x 3.30in)

Compression ratio

998cc 8.3:1 (8.9:1 with automatic)
1,098cc 8.5:1

Maximum power

998cc 38bhp @ 5,250rpm (automatic: 41bhp @ 4,850rpm)
1,098cc 45bhp @ 5,250rpm

Maximum torque

998cc 52lb ft (70Nm) @ 2,700rpm (automatic 2,750rpm)
1,098cc 56lb ft (76Nm) @ 2,700rpm

Carburettor

Single 1¼in SU HS2

TRANSMISSION

Gearbox

Four-speed all synchromesh. Optional Automotive Products four-speed automatic, only with 998cc engine

Ratios	Standard	Close ratio
1st	3.63:1	2.69:1
2nd	2.17:1	1.845:1
3rd	1.412:1	1.46:1
Top	1.000:1	1.000:1
Reverse	3.63:1	2.69:1

Clutch

Borg and Beck, 7⅛in diaphragm spring

Final drive

Helical spur gears, ratios: manual 3.44:1, automatic 3.27:1

BRAKES

Front

Lockheed drum, 7in x 1¼in

Rear

Lockheed drum, 7in x 1¼in

Operation

Lockheed hydraulic

Handbrake

Lever, with cable linkage to rear drums

SUSPENSION

Front

Independent, Hydrolastic suspension units with hydraulic connection to rear suspension (rubber cone springs, no interconnection, from mid-1971), double wishbones, telescopic dampers

Rear

Independent, Hydrolastic suspension units with hydraulic connection to front suspension (rubber cone springs, no inter connection, from mid-1971), trailing arms, telescopic dampers

STEERING

Type

Rack and pinion

Number of turns lock to lock

2⅓

Turning circle

28ft 6in (8.7m)

Steering wheel

Three spoke, 15in diameter

WHEELS AND TYRES

Steel disc wheels, 3½J x 10in (4½J x 12in with Denovo tyres from 1977)

Tyres

998cc 5.20-10in cross-ply
1,098cc 145-10in radial-ply
(Optional Dunlop Denovo run-flat tyres on 12in wheels)

PERFORMANCE

Autocar road tests: 998cc 16 December 1971; 1,098cc 27 November 1976

Top speed

998cc 75mph (120kph)
1,098cc 82mph (132kph)

Acceleration

0–30mph (48kph)	5.1sec	5.9sec
0–50mph (80kph)	14.1sec	12.4sec
0–60mph (96kph)	21.0sec	17.9sec
Standing quarter mile (402m)	21.9sec	20.7sec

Overall fuel consumption

998cc 34.5mpg (8.2l/100km)
1,098cc 37.2mpg (7.6l/100km)

DIMENSIONS

Length

10ft 4⅜in (3,165mm)

Width

4ft 7½in (1,410mm)

Height

4ft 5in (1,346mm)

Wheelbase

6ft 8½in (2,036mm)

Track

Front: 4ft 0in (1,219 mm)
Rear: 3ft 11¼in (1,200mm)

Ground Clearance

7⅛in (181mm)

Unladen weight

1,406lb (638kg)

1966–1993
The Innocenti Minis

Innocenti was founded in Milan in 1933 as a steel pressings business. Postwar it made Lambretta scooters and linked up with BMC in 1960 to produce the Austin A40 Farina. A specially styled Sprite in 1961 was followed by manufacture of the front-wheel-drive BMC1100 (called IM3) and the first Minis were built from 1965. Until the 1970s all these cars were sold only in Italy.

When Ferdinand Innocenti died in 1972 British Leyland bought the business, renaming it Leyland Innocenti SpA, and Innocenti Minis were henceforth assembled in Spain and Belgium. In 1974 came the Mini 90 and Mini 120 Bertone-styled hatchbacks.

By 1973 Innocenti was making over 60,000 cars a year but BL's financial crisis in 1975 forced Leyland-Innocenti into liquidation. This killed off the UK-based cars but entrepreneur Alejandro de Tomaso bought the business and put the Bertone cars on sale. These Mini De Tomasos sold in large numbers (220,000 in all) until 1982, when De Tomaso relaunched and renamed the cars using Daihatsu engines and transmissions.

Italian flair and better equipment

The first time I drove an Innocenti-built Mini-Cooper, I wondered why BMC couldn't produce the same sort of car in the UK. Although it didn't go any better than a British-built type, it was better trimmed and better equipped – and somehow there was a whiff of Italian flair. When I asked about Innocenti models at this time, and the possibility of them being sold in the UK, the idea was airily dismissed. British buyers, it was suggested, didn't want the extra equipment and certainly wouldn't pay for the Innocenti versions.

However, the Italians would – and did. So why did the Italians deserve a facia like that, those neat little 1275GT-style wheels, and front doors with swivelling quarter lights, when the Brits couldn't have them? The Italians loved the cars, of course. In the 1960s and 1970s, when Italy's major cities were not as crowded as they are now, I can remember scudding round the streets of Turin and Milan in small Fiats but sometimes having to give best to the Italian-registered Minis, which challenged every traffic light, roundabout, and overtaking opportunity.

The Italian-built Mini was a great success in Italy. Innocenti's factory built more than 50,000 Minis almost every year from 1966 1974, sometimes as many as 300 cars a day. The Italians had no hang-ups about this being a foreign car – the Mini, after all, was international currency. *The Italian Job* had not only done a great publicity job for the little box but it had also glorified the backdrop of Turin and – what the hell – this was an Italian-built car!

Left: Cars badged as Innocenti Mini-Coopers were built in Italy in large numbers, these not only having different decorative details at the front but wind-up door windows too.

Minis in Fiat territory

n the 1960s, not even Fiat could match what Alec Issigonis had achieved. Facing up to the Mini, the rear-engined 600s and 850s were struggling. They might have been cheaper but they didn't look as good, they didn't handle as well, and didn't go as quickly either. For a time, though, Fiat could afford to be complacent, for Italian-market Minis had o be shipped from the UK and numbers were quite small. Now Innocenti decided o fight Fiat head-on, for the small-car market, by putting the Mini into production in Milan.

It was a pragmatic deal, the most successful overseas manufacturing project that BMC ever tackled. The first Innocenti Minis used running gear and some body panels shipped from Longbridge but Innocenti pressed the rest and manufactured all the trim parts in Italy. At first this was a straightforward commercial arrangement, with Innocenti building cars to sell in Italy while BMC carried on selling to all other European territories.

Then, as later, Innocenti Minis were always that bit extra special, with a higher specification and Italian-only features like special grilles and badges, side indicator lamps, reversing lamps, and other details. Estate car versions were added from 1966.

Until 1968, and the arrival of the MkII models, Innocenti Minis were mechanically the same as UK Minis. After that the 848cc engines were given 9.0:1 compression ratios with a 1½in SU HS4 carburettor and were rated at 48bhp (gross) – about 42bhp (net): this allowed Innocenti to claim an 84mph top speed, just about enough to keep up with the Fiats in the traffic light Grand Prix.

(Innocenti always quoted the maximum possible horsepower – test bed (gross) rather

Opposite: Recognise this badge? Thought not – for it appeared on Mini-Coopers built by Innocenti in Italy.

Above: Although the Innocenti Mini-Cooper was never officially marketed in the UK, a number of such cars were imported privately – as confirmed by this British-registered example.

than installed (net) – so that it could match similarly optimistic claims from Italian manufacturers. This makes it difficult to compare the cars with UK horsepower ratings.)

That was the year in which the first Innocenti Mini-Cooper appeared. Basically this was a 998cc Mini-Cooper with twin SU HS2 carbs but once again there were differences – sculptured wheel styles, radial-ply tyres as standard, Cooper S-size front disc brakes, a 9.5:1 compression ratio engine, and peak power rated at 60bhp (gross): this time the top speed claim was 93mph.

The Mark III types followed in 1970, not only with the concealed-door-hinge body

style and wind-up windows but with swivelling front quarterlights in the doors (just like the arrangement already found in Australian-built cars).

Although British cars had all reverted to rubber cone suspension by then, Innocentis retained Hydrolastic suspension for a time. An automatic transmission (Mini-Matic) appeared at this time, while for the Mini-Cooper there was a new type of facia, a full-width style with five circular dials: this, though, was not logical, for the speedometer and rev counter were in the centre of the display, the three auxiliary instruments being ahead of the driver's eyes!

By the early 1970s, please note, the Cooper name had disappeared from UK-

market Minis but Innocenti would retain it until the very end of production in 1975/1976. Not only that but no sooner had the British Mini-Cooper 1275S been dropped in 1971 than Innocenti prepared to launch its own version!

The Leyland Innocenti Mini-Cooper 1300, and the Mini-Cooper 1300 Export which followed it, both used the same type of 1,275cc engine. Although both had the familiar twin semi-downdraught SU carburettor layout, these were not Mini-Cooper S engines but a later, less highly-tuned, hybrid version – more closely related to, say, the twin-SU engines being fitted to British-market MG 1300 MkIIs of the period!

The 1300 Export was the most highly developed of all Minis at the time. Introduced in 1973 (and soon also manufactured at British Leyland plants in Spain and Belgium), not only did this car get yet another new facia style – this time with a six-dial instrument layout, the speedometer and rev counter still being in the centre – but there were the latest rod-type gear change linkage, dual-circuit brakes, 1275GT-style road wheels, unique badging and grille styles. In addition, there were larger pedals and a leather-rimmed, alloy-spoked, steering wheel.

By any Mini standards these were desirable little cars, as fast as any unmodified Mini-Cooper S yet with their own distinctive style features. Because so many of them were made – no fewer than 28,200 in a mere two years – there was an excellent supply for import by British enthusiasts. Once the first cars were imported, by the way, several subtle panel differences became obvious – particularly the boot lid with its different recess for the Italian-shape registration plate.

In Italy, as in the UK, the Mini-Cooper was finally killed off by events it could not control. In the UK it was because Lord Stokes would not extend John Cooper's royalty agreement, while in Italy it was because the business closed down around the car itself.

Even then, of course, there was more to come, for the Bertone-styled hatchback car then took over.

Power comparisons

As I have already noted, because of the different method of quoting power outputs, comparisons can only be a guide:

	UK Mini-Cooper S	Innocenti Mini-Cooper 1300 Export
Engine size	1,275cc	1,275cc
Compression ratio	9.75:1	9.75:1
Power	76bhp (net) @ 5,800rpm	71bhp (gross) @ 5,800rpm
Torque	79lb ft at 3,000rpm	79.5lb ft at 3,200rpm

Even though the power was slightly down from that of the 1275S, Innocenti still claimed a top speed of 95mph.

Left: Innocenti not only assembled Mini-Coopers in Italy but progressively modified them. This was one of the different facia/instrument layouts fitted over the years.

The Bertone hatchback

In a development that confused Mini-watchers for years, an Italian giant and a related styling house – Bertone – had become involved with the Mini. At the Turin Motor Show in November 1974, Innocenti showed a new model: the Innocenti Mini.

British Leyland approved of this project – it was to supply underbody platforms and all the running gear – and there were rumours that this was also a kite-flying exercise from home. Not so – Innocenti, in cahoots with Bertone, had gained British Leyland's approval to start this as a private-enterprise project.

Innocenti had the size, the capability, and the industrial muscle to commission its own pressed-steel bodyshell and tooling but not the style, so it turned to Bertone for that. Though it used virtually unmodified Mini platform and bulkhead assemblies, plus the well-known A-series engine, transmission and running gear, Innocenti then completed a remarkably attractive new superstructure.

The overall length was 123in – three inches longer than the original – while the width had crept up to 59in. The lines were altogether smarter and more crisp than those of the original, there was a rear hatchback/third-door and folding rear seats.

Innocenti produced this car in 998cc '90' and 1,275cc '120' form – both engines being allied to a front-mounted water radiator with an electric fan. Both had far more luxurious equipment than on standard cars being built in the UK: 120 models had a full-width facia, face-level ventilation, reclining front seats, and a rear wash/wipe was standard.

Although these pretty little cars were no more spacious than the originals, and were considerably more expensive, they had panache and soon began to sell very well. So, why was the Bertone style not adopted at Longbridge?

Designer Harris Mann, explained all: 'The problem was the seating package. There was not more, but less, room inside than in a Mini, and that would never have done. Charles Griffin [who had recently become Director of Engineering] had laid

down a minimum package for the new car, and the Bertone was a long way off.'

British interest in the Bertone Mini, therefore, died almost as soon as it had been born. Although British Leyland imported a few cars and considered their use very carefully, the idea of transplanting assembly to the UK was soon abandoned. The Bertone-styled car, though, went on to a long and distinguished career. After British Leyland's bankruptcy in 1975,

Innocenti was bought by Alejandro de Tomaso (whose other interests already included Maserati). From 1976 the Mini was rebadged as the De Tomaso Mini and carried on strongly. In 1982 it was completely re-engineered with a Daihatsu 993cc three-cylinder power pack, though the Mini platform and suspension layouts were always retained. Eventually Fiat bought Nuova Innocenti and the last Mini-based car was built in 1993.

Above: Bertone's crisp styling for the Innocenti Mini (this is the 120 version) was quite different from the BMC original and had a third door and folding rear seats.

Opposite: Innocenti Minis in mass production in Milan in 1974, showing just how serious the Italians were about making a success of this Bertone-styled machine. Note the Mini-Cooper assembly line behind.

Innocenti Mini production

Total Innocenti Mini production, from 1965 to 1976, was approximately 450,000. Of this total, the following were Mini-Coopers:

Model	Years	Cars built
Mini-Cooper MkI	1966–1968	12,800
Mini-Cooper MkII	1968–1970	9,000
Mini-Cooper MkIII	1970–1972	15,500
Mini-Cooper 1300	1972–1973	10,000
Leyland-Innocenti Mini-Cooper1300 Export	1973–1975	28,200

ROVER MINI &
MINI-COOPER
1990–2000

1990–1996 New Rover Coopers and Cabriolets

In May 1989, Mini enthusiasts greeted one modest piece of news from the Rover Group almost as reverently as the Second Coming. This was that, for the first time in 18 years, Longbridge had once again given official approval to 'Cooper' being linked with 'Mini'. Although this was only approval of a performance kit at first, more important developments were already on the way.

In 1989, though, the reborn Cooper was very different – for even the names had all been changed. Longbridge, the home of the Mini, was still there and, although it was ageing faster than the investment could catch up, it was now a vastly different place. British Leyland had died, discredited, in the late 1970s, Austin-Rover had followed, and a company called the Rover Group had taken its place: not only that but since 1988 Rover had been owned by the British Aerospace Group.

Politics of the reborn Mini-Cooper

When British Leyland's much-loved Mini-Cooper 1275S had been killed off in mid-1971, most of us thought it was the end of a distinguished career for that sort of car. British Leyland's management wanted rid of anything on which it had to pay royalties – John Cooper most deservedly earned one on every car built – and was (wrongly) convinced that the 1275GT would do the same image-building job for the Mini.

Out there, though, you – the customer – wouldn't let it die and kept on nagging for a return. It took time, so it was nearly 20 years later that a new generation of Longbridge management was persuaded to dig out the old files, blow off the

Right: Even before Rover reintroduced the Mini-Cooper in 1990, it backed the John Cooper Performance Conversion Kit – which featured twin SU carburettors on a 998cc engine. The power output was 64bhp and the conversion cost £995, plus tax and fitting charges.

dust from the old marketing profiles – and to relaunch the Cooper badge!

However, most of Longbridge management's old Mini-Cooper enthusiasts had moved on and the Mini (though still being made on the same old facilities and the same old assembly lines) had become a marginalised model, quite overshadowed by the Metro and other Honda-inspired front-wheel-drive machines.

Because there were still many profit-obsessed people at Rover who thought the Mini should already have been dropped completely (in the late 1980s, personal interest from British Aerospace's Graham Day had had much to do with its survival), management had to be very canny. This is why the very first batch of 'new' Mini-Coopers would be officially approved conversions of ordinary Minis, twin-carburetted 998cc-engined cars to be built by John Cooper in 1989, the very apposite excuse being that this was to commemorate the Mini's 30th anniversary. This conversion, incidentally, was only available on manual

transmission cars which had no catalytic converter fitted.

When Britain's *Autocar* tested a car, it headlined its feature 'Return of the White Roof' and (although this car only had 64bhp) cooed over the increase in performance and character. Maybe a top speed of just 85mph and 0–60mph in 13.2sec merely put this car back on a par with the Mini-Cooper of the 1960s but who

was counting? Cast alloy wheels, a three-spoke alloy steering wheel, a bit of wheel-spin if and when you were lucky, the white roof, and the special livery (which included stripes along the side and rear decals) made it all worthwhile. All of which came at a rather stiff price – for the conversion, which was carried out at John Cooper's premises at Ferring, in West Sussex, cost £1,466.

Above: As re-launched in 1990, the Mini-Cooper looked subtly different from its predecessor of the early 1970s.

Series-production Mini-Coopers

That, though, was only a start, for Rover had plans to start building Cooper-badged Minis at Longbridge once again. The very first of the official new-generation 1,275cc-engined Mini-Coopers was launched in July 1990 and was based on the Mini Thirty special edition.

However, although the name was the same as in the 1960s, the technical specification was widely different from that of those earlier models – as the comparison table makes clear. Although the basic bodyshell was the same as before, everything from the engine, to the

transmission, the suspension, brakes, and body equipment had 'grown up' in the intervening decades.

All cars were intended to have Minilite-clone alloy wheels, wheelarch extensions, and the famous white roof panel over contrasting body colours: in addition, the original batch not only came with the traditional racing type of angled white bonnet stripes, plus a 'John Cooper' signature, but a glass sunroof and auxiliary driving lamps too.

Because of the impact of the latest noise and exhaust emissions regulations, recently

Nearly 20 years after British Leyland had killed off the Mini-Cooper badge, Rover reintroduced the car, this time with a single-carburettor 1,275cc engine. The original limited-edition type of 1990 had 'John Cooper' signatures on the bonnet stripes.

Below: The story goes that when John Cooper heard of the 1,650-off Limited Edition which was to be reintroduced, he thought he would have to sign the bonnet of each and every car!

Right: Although everyone calls these alloy wheels 'Minilites' (after the style first seen on 'works' rally cars in the 1960s) they were actually made by another manufacturer as the trademark rights had lapsed. All 1990s-style Mini-Coopers had such wheels.

Far left: The revived Mini-Cooper of 1990 featured these elaborately detailed plastic mouldings, which were all intended to keep water out of the distributor and off the plug leads of the A-series engine.

Left: The 1990 Mini-Cooper had large, body colour, door mirrors – later cars would have mirrors matching the roof colour instead.

Below: The easy way to 'pick' the reintroduced Mini-Cooper of the 1990s was by the badging on the boot lid and the rear flanks. No sheet metal changes were ever made to this model.

implemented, the cars had to be fitted with single-carburettor 1,275cc engines so that they could produce acceptable performance and a clean exhaust. Tyres were low-profile 165/60R-12in Dunlop SP Sports.

Rover originally suggested that only 1,000 of the first limited-edition cars (which cost £6,995) would be produced before 'regular production' began in September but in the end no fewer than 1,650 of those cars were made.

From September 1990, the standard specification was slimmed down – unhappily for collectors, the white bonnet stripes, the sunroof, the John Cooper signatures, and the driving lamps had all been deleted (though most remained as optional extras and were often ordered – yes, confusing, isn't it!). Steering wheels and carpets were black instead of the limited-edition car's red.

For the next 13 months, this production car (generally known as Mini-Cooper Carb) was freely available – at first for £6,595 – and right from the start at least one in three of all Minis being built at Longbridge in the early 1990s was Cooper-badged. Compared with the 1960s, when the entire Mini-Cooper image was new, the 1990s model was not as excitingly different but there was still a healthy demand for a car that looked so sporting. Maybe it was the badge, maybe it was the wheels and maybe it was the stripes – but buyers seemed to love the new cars.

Right: Familiar driving position, but different trim and equipment, of a 1990 Mini-Cooper. This early-type Limited Edition featured the red-rimmed wheel and the black leather seating.

Opposite: No more and no less space in the front compartment of the 1990 Mini-Cooper than ever before.

Below right: Still not much space for pedals, even on the 1990-type Mini-Cooper, with front wheelarches intruding as usual.

Below: Three instrument dials, neatly packaged ahead of the driver's eyes, of the 1990 Mini-Cooper – a logical evolution of those seen on 1275GTs and special edition cars of the 1980s.

Below: The first 1,650 Mini-Coopers, all built in 1990, featured black leather trim and these neat little 'Mini-Cooper' inserts on the seats.

Bottom: When revived, the Mini-Cooper carried its identification proudly on the horn button in the centre of the steering wheel.

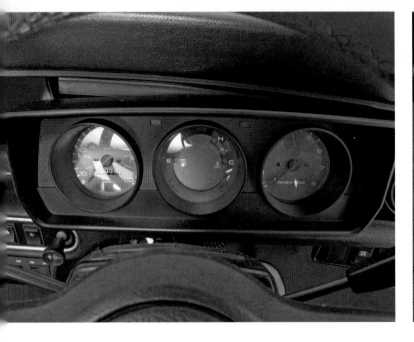

Within months John Cooper's latest Mini-Cooper S conversion had gone on sale – not built at Longbridge but converted in Sussex – this adding 15bhp, and 10mph to the top speed, all helped along with twin SU carburettors and a reworked cylinder head, for the rather hefty conversion price of £1,751. The performance of that car was almost identical to that of the legendary factory-built Mini-Cooper 1275S of the 1960s. If one was feeling really rich, a 'handling kit' was also available for an extra £671.

Such a car could only be created by the customer actually taking his own car (newly-registered and usually barely just-run-in) to a Rover dealer or to John Cooper at Worthing, handing it over for conversion, then waiting for the work to be done, so demand was actually quite limited.

Right: From 1990 the Mini-Cooper had these badges on the boot lid and on the rear quarters. While British Leyland couldn't wait to drop the 'Cooper' name in 1971, Rover was delighted to have it back in 1990.

Right: Totally different to 1970s-type badging, this was the way that the 1990 Mini-Cooper was identified on the bonnet.

Mini-Cooper in 1990: old and new compared

Original-generation Mini-Coopers were built from 1961 to 1969. New-generation Rover Mini-Coopers were launched in 1990. The two types were very different. Here's a thumbnail comparison between two of the most typical models:

	Mini-Cooper 998cc	Rover Mini-Cooper 1.3
Announced	1964	1990
Body	Sliding door windows, central instruments, 5½-gallon fuel tank	Wind-up windows, instruments ahead of driver, 7½-gallon fuel tank
Engine	998cc, 55bhp Two SU carburettors	1,275cc, 61bhp One SU carburettor
Transmission	No synchro on 1st gear	All synchromesh
Suspension	Hydrolastic from late 1964	Rubber cone springs
Brakes	7in front discs, no servo as standard	8.4in front discs, servo
Wheels	3½J-10in	4½J-12in
Tyres	145-10in radial-ply	145/70-12in radial-ply
Weight	1,400lb	1,535lb
Top speed	87mph	92mph
UK price	£568 (1964)	£6,995 (1990)

Below: Mini-Cooper, 1990-style. The alloy wheels emphasised the sporting heritage.

The first fuel-injected Minis

Whether standard or modified, though, these were new Minis to remind everyone just how much fun it could still be to drive a tiny car as rapidly as the tyres would allow. The standard car might not have been dramatically faster than the City or the Mayfair but it certainly felt like it – and no one could miss the extrovert style that went with the new badge.

Because of the way that exhaust emission regulations, worldwide, were still closing in on the Mini, the Mini-Cooper had to be upgraded for the 1992 model year. From October 1991, the Mini-Cooper 1.3i took over from the earlier type, that magic letter 'i' showing that the engine had been fitted with single-point Lucas fuel injection. Engineers will understand why it was something of a miracle that an engine whose design roots lay in the 1950s should still be capable of being 'cleaned up' to meet 1990s standards.

As far as the Mini-Cooper was concerned,

Above: When Rover relaunched the Mini-Cooper brand in 1990, it also released a picture showing the new type in comparison to a Mini-Cooper MkII of 1967. Not too many visual differences, right?

Left: Russ Swift, that master of two-wheel driving, always put on a splendid display with this trio of Mini-Coopers in the 1990s. Don't try this at home...

Above: The Mini-Cooper 1.3i, with fuel injection, replaced the original carburetted type at the end of 1991.

Right: Some Mini interiors were starker than others, this car being kitted out for pure competition work.

this was a 'first' (other Mini models would follow suit a year later), especially as space had somehow been found underneath the virtually flat floorpan for a three-way catalytic converter. Although the cost went up yet again – to £7,845 (£720 more than before) in October 1991 – it wasn't all bad news, for the quoted peak power for factory-built engines actually edged up from 61bhp to 63bhp, the top speed eased up to over 90mph once again, and those extra driving lamps crept back into the standard specification. There was, in other words, still enough novelty in the life of the Mini/Mini-Cooper to keep specification 'anoraks' in business.

Unhappily, what the Mini-Cooper 1.3i really needed to bring it into the 1990s was

Right: Four Coopers in one shot: Father John, son Mike, and two Mini-Cooper 1.3is, pictured in 1995. Mike later went on to forge links with BMW for a new-generation MINI-Cooper.

a five-speed gearbox but this could not be provided in the existing gearbox-in-sump layout and there was never any likelihood of the installation being reworked (as it had been in the Metro of the period) to make this possible. Not that this seemed to deter the customers, who went out and bought the cars just as often as their fathers had done in the 1960s, for there was just as much grip as ever (the 165/60R-12 Dunlops saw to that) and if anyone had ever invented more tactile steering for a car, then it had never been put on sale.

As with the earlier car, John Cooper developed an even hotter Mini-Cooper Si version, this time retaining the fuel injection but with 77bhp and a top speed of just about 100mph.

after Paddy Hopkirk's famous victory in 33 EJB, the 'works' 1071S: Paddy, in fact, was persuaded to drive one of the cars himself.

To commemorate this Rover also built a series of Monte Carlo 'dress-up kit' cars in January 1994, followed by a special Mini Monte Carlo in July 1994, which had a modified interior with a wooden facia, gunmetal alloy wheels, and a bank of four extra driving lamps, rally-style, across the front grille: this glitzy car cost £7,995.

In mid-1995 wider wheels (6J width, 175/50 tyres) were standardised, along with a wooden facia but there was still more to come. Before the major changes which would follow in October 1996 (which included multi-point fuel injection – this all being described in the next chapter), the last of the special 'dress-up kit' Mini-Coopers to be introduced, in May 1996, was the Mini-Cooper 35, of which only 200 were built at £8,195 each. As with the Monte Carlo cars, there was a line of driving lamps across the nose and dark painted alloy wheels. Like the original 1961 cars, the '35' was painted Almond Green (with a green interior). After that the Mini-Cooper was reborn for 1997, this time with a multi-point fuel-injected engine and a lot more. The Mini story still had four more years to run at the historic Longbridge factory.

Left: John Cooper, father of the entire Mini-Cooper brand, was delighted to see the famous car brought back into production in the 1990s. Here he is seen in a 1.3i of 1995, which was complete with optional extras including leather upholstery.

Bottom left: In the 1990s, the revived Mini-Cooper only had one fuel tank – the enlarged 7½ gallon variety as used on other models by this time.

Below: To celebrate 35 years of the Mini Cooper, John Cooper (right) and celebrated race driver John Rhodes posed alongside this Cooper 35 special edition, which was decked out in Almond Green paint.

At this point the mechanical specification settled down for the next few years, though there were other specification changes to follow. A trim update of March 1993 included new-type front seats, an internal bonnet release only 34 years after the original external-release type had gone on sale), a passenger-side door mirror, and an engine alarm/immobiliser.

By this time Rover was so fired up about the rebirth of the Mini-Cooper that it supported the entry of 'works' cars in the 1994 Monte Carlo Rally, though these were built outside the factory, which had very little influence on their specification. The choice of 1994 is easy enough to explain – it was just 30 years

City, Mayfair, and Sprite for the 1990s

At Longbridge, although all the excitement of this period was being created by the reborn Mini-Cooper, the City and Mayfair models continued as steadily as ever. As the 1990s opened, there were two 998cc-engined models in the range: the entry-level City and the more upmarket Mayfair. Both had 42bhp engines, optional automatic transmission, 12in wheels, and servo-assisted front-wheel disc brakes.

By 1982, when the City disappeared in favour of a newly badged car, the Sprite, nearly 1.5 million of these ADO20 types had built since the start of assembly in 1969; when they disappeared that also signalled the end of the 998cc engine in the Mini shell.

Launched in May 1992, two new models badged Sprite and Mayfair were both fitted with 50bhp 1,275cc single-carburettor engines. Sprite was a name with a long and varied history in the BMC/British Leyland/Rover heritage: first used on a Riley sports car in the 1930s, it had then been used on an Austin-Healey sports car in the 1960s, and as recently as 1983 for a special edition Mini.

The Sprite replaced the City as the entry-level Mini of the day: it retailed at £5,753, while the revised Mayfair cost £6,932. Automatic transmission, optional on both models, cost £965 – because this was seen to be expensive, it attracted a very limited demand.

Sprites picked up most old-type City features, which included black plastic wheelarch extensions and chrome bumpers. By contrast, the latest Mayfair had a new Mini-Cooper-like grille, more upmarket trim and equipment, which included velour seat facings, a two-instrument facia pack, and the option of Cooper-style cast-alloy road wheels.

As ever, improvements came regularly:

May 1993 Larger Metro-style front seats, an internal bonnet release (for the first time), and (on the Mayfair only) a full-width walnut dashboard containing three instruments.

August 1994 On both cars, to allow them to meet the latest exhaust emission regulations, single-point fuel injection replaced the SU carburettor, this also helping to nudge the peak power up to 53bhp at 5,000rpm and the top speed from 87mph to 88mph.

June 1995 In what would be the last update on this generation of Minis, both cars gained black carpeting, rear-seat inertia-reel safety belts (to match those at the front), a remote-activated alarm/immobiliser system, and another set of enhanced trim and seating details.

By this time, total Mini production at Longbridge had settled down to its lowest-ever level. While 26,197 cars had been built in 1992, less than 20,500 cars would be built in each of the next three seasons. Although there was still a demand out there, it was no longer as high as in the glory days of the 1960s and 1970s. Not even the long-awaited introduction of an open-top model had helped reverse that trend.

Rover Mini-Cooper 1.3i and its rivals in 1991

Make and model	Top speed	0–60mph	Standing ¼ mile	Fuel consumption	Price inc tax
Citroën AX GT	107mph	9.0sec	16.8sec	30mpg	£8,885
Daihatsu Charade GTi	114mph	7.9sec	16.4sec	29mpg	£9,340
Fiat Uno Turbo ie	126mph	8.3sec	16.4sec	26mpg	£10,939
Ford Fiesta XR2i	118mph	8.9sec	16.7sec	28mpg	£10,522
Rover Mini-Cooper 1.3i	92mph	11.5sec	–	32mpg	£7,845
Suzuki Swift 1.3GTi	114mph	8.7sec	16.8sec	29mpg	£8,199

A soft-top Mini – at last

When it came to designing the Mini in 1957/1958, BMC's Chairman, Sir Leonard Lord, gave Alec Issigonis a very restricted brief. For the first few years at least, Issigonis and his team had to develop a one-track mind and frivolities like open-top Minis would have to wait.

Except for the Mini-Moke that wait turned into more than 30 years – 30 years, in fairness, at Longbridge, though not by private concerns such as Crayford, which had it sussed in the early 1960s. The first successful drop-top Mini to be announced was the original Crayford of mid-1963.

By the end of the 1980s, the motoring world was beginning to treat the classic Mini like the pet Labrador – we would smile indulgently whenever we saw one, pat it on the head, but require no more than love and affection, for there was nothing to surprise us. Until 1991, that is, when Rover's marketing staff suddenly decided that open-air motoring was attractive. Not only did it approve a Mini drop-top but also produced Metro and Rover 200 Cabriolet concepts too. Although the craze was short-lived, the Mini-based car eventually made it to the marketplace.

German enterprise

It was the German Rover dealer, LAMM Autohaus, which actually produced the first very smart-looking convertible officially backed by Rover and eventually put it on sale through 12 Rover outlets in Britain. Starting out on the basis of a contemporary fuel-injected Rover Cooper, LAMM contracted Karmann, the German cabriolet/body conversion specialists to engineer the job and to modify, re-equip, and manufacture the production bodyshells.

As you might expect, Karmann was instructed to leave the running gear well alone. Concentrating entirely on the bodyshell, the coachbuilders carved off the roof and rear quarter panels, made extensive changes (out of sight) to the sills and B/C posts (behind the doors), and added a new floor cross-member, all to help retain rigidity.

The external body/dress-up kit included enormous 175/50 tyres on five-spoke Revolution alloys, big wheelarch extensions to cover them, sills along the flanks, and a front chin spoiler (with in-built driving lamps), all linked to an upmarket interior including a wood-grain facia, gear-lever knob, and door cappings, along with a Cooper-style leather steering wheel. Somehow, because of those fat wheels, arches, and sills, the LAMM convertible looked a whole lot bigger than the Mini saloon on which it was based,

Above: It took the Mini's owners 32 years before they finally approved the building of a convertible derivative – this being the Cabriolet of 1991.

Left: The Cabriolet, introduced in 1991, was still a four-seater, but there was no way of hiding the soft-top when it was folded back.

though in reality it was no longer and perhaps 130lb heavier.

The soft-top itself was voluminous, and sat up in a big bag when furled, but rear seat space was just as much as in the saloon (that doesn't often happen with other convertibles). Only one colour was available – Cherry red, with a maroon soft-top – but at an all-in price of £12,250 the British allocation of just 75 right-hand-drive cars soon sold out. Many more left-hand-drive LAMM cars were sold in Germany throughout the 1990s.

At £12,250 one might have expected this project to fail miserably, for at the time a Mini-Cooper saloon cost £6,947. The Cabriolet, therefore, cost 76 per cent more than the saloon – in the 1960s such an impost would have killed it off, stone dead, at birth but in the 1990s there were any number of trendies who saw the Mini as a real retro-classic, even while it was still on sale.

Below: The Cabriolet was substantially re-engineered, not only around the cabin but with wider-than-ever wheelarch extensions, special alloy wheels, and very sturdy matching bumper mouldings.

Longbridge replies

To their credit, Longbridge's planners seemed to have reacted quickly to the reception gained by the LAMM Cabriolet. Only 16 months later, Rover announced its own version of that car, claiming that Rover Special Products had been involved in the launch of its own model, which was 'very different' from the LAMM car.

That, of course, was a typical motor industry 'smoke and mirrors' exercise, for the latest Cabriolet was no more than a significantly updated evolution of the LAMM car. Once again, Karmann would produce the bodyshells, though this time final assembly would be at Longbridge itself.

Try as I might, except for the update to 63bhp (which all Coopers got at about this time) and the fitment of an alarm system to deter the British knuckle-draggers from taking away something

which was not theirs, I can see very little visual or technical difference between the LAMM (German) or Longbridge (British-built) convertibles. Interesting, of course – doesn't time fly in this industry? – that there were no safety roll-hoops behind the seats (look at today's MINI Convertible to see what is meant), no steering wheel air bag, and no ABS brakes either. You could, on the other hand, order a power-operated soft-top if you wanted to up the price...

Longbridge-built Cabriolets finally went on sale in July 1993 – almost 34 years after the original Mini went on sale, had it really taken so long? The latest car was available in a choice of colours (Caribbean Blue or Nightfire Red, both with red soft-top fabrics, at first, with British Racing Green added later) and had its soft-top mechanism made by Tickford. This time around, too, there had been a slight reduction in price, for the Longbridge car retailed at £11,995 (in mid-1993 the Cooper saloon cost £6,995, so the gap had been closed to just 71 per cent!). Rover said it was hoping to produce up to 15 cars every week – about 700 cars in a full year – but the customer rush to the showrooms never materialised.

All that extra bodyshell stiffening and equipment had made the Convertible heavier – 1,654lb instead of 1,521lb – so it didn't accelerate as fast as the saloon. Rover claimed a top speed of 92mph, with 0–60mph in just 12.3sec but the fatter tyres gave more cornering grip and made up for that.

After the initial publicity rush, the Convertible soon became a forgotten car – this was hardly surprising. It wasn't just that the Convertible's time had gone – it was that the classic Mini itself was well on the way to retirement. By 1996 BMW was in control of Rover, sales of Longbridge-built cars had reached only 700 examples, and newly built Convertibles were rarely seen on the assembly lines at Longbridge. When the classic Mini received its last major revamp in 1996, the Convertible was quietly laid to rest.

Limited editions

As in the 1970s and 1980s, there was a positive torrent of special editions in the 1990s. These, of course, were produced to keep up the interest in a car which otherwise had very little novelty to offer at the time. As with the earlier 'specials', the ground rules were that special editions should look much more different than they actually were. Under the skin, there would always be familiar components but visually they sometimes had a complete makeover.

In all cases except one (the LAMM-built Cabriolet, which I have already described), the company's special-edition Minis were based on the familiar short-nose two-door saloon. All cars listed below had 998cc engines unless otherwise stated. In some cases one feature or fitting was used for the very first time on a Mini (but was maybe adopted later as a 'mainstream' fitment). In that case, I have listed it here under

'Innovations'. This, I think, is a complete list of UK-market special-edition Minis produced from 1990 to 1996 inclusive. All of them had wheelarch extensions.

1990 Racing Green/Flame Red/Check Mate (City): Green, red, or black, all with white roof, plus Minilite-style wheels. Priced at £5,455, with £895 for optional automatic transmission. Just 2,500 for UK customers, many more exported. Innovations: 3.44:1 final drive (ex-Mini-Cooper S), Rover-approved John Cooper performance kit. Studio 2 (City): Black, Nordic Blue, or Storm Grey, plus Doeskin seat covers. Priced at £5,375 with 2,000 for UK.

Mini-Cooper (Thirty, ex-Mayfair): Forerunner of reintroduced Mini-Cooper series production car and already mentioned above. Cost £6,995 with 1,000 cars produced. Innovations: 1,275cc engine, first-ever usage in a non-Cooper-S Mini.
1991 Neon (City): Nordic Blue, plus Chevron velour trim. Cost £5,570 with 1,500 produced.
Cabriolet (Mini-Cooper): Convertible, completed by LAMM of Germany, as already described above. Cost £12,250 but only 75 sold in the UK. Innovations: First-ever factory-approved drop-top Mini, not constructed in the UK, 175/50-12in tyres/wheels.

1992 British Open Classic (Mayfair 1.3): British Racing Green. Priced at £7,195 with 1,000 for the UK. Innovations: Electrically operated fold-back sunroof. Italian Job (Sprite): The obvious inspiration – though a somewhat lengthy 23 years after the original *The Italian Job* film was released. Four different paint schemes: Flame Red, Diamond White, British Racing Green metallic, and Electric Blue, with contrasting roof colour. Sold for £5,995, with 1,000 for the UK market and 750 for Italy. Innovations: Reversion to a 1960s-style Morris Mini-Minor grille, two additional driving lamps.

Above: Three special editions: the Flame, Checkmate, and Racing all came together in February 1990, just in time to arouse interest in the mainstream Mini-Cooper.

Middle left: The Mini British Open Classic was a limited edition with a tenuous connection to the annual golf classic event held in the UK. One important feature was the full-length fold-back sunroof.

Middle right: The Mini Italian Job special edition, launched in October 1992, was available in one of four different colours. It looked faster than it was, for the engine was a standard 50bhp/1,275cc power unit.

1993 Rio (Sprite): Three colour schemes. Cost £5,495 with 750 cars built for UK. Tahiti (Sprite): Painted in pearlescent Tahiti Blue. Priced at £5,795, or £6,715 with automatic transmission, 500 cars built for UK.

1994 Monte Carlo (Mini-Cooper): Rally dress-up kit, not a true special edition, for £7,195. Innovations: Rally number patches on doors, four driving lamps (two more than standard car).
Mini 35 (Sprite): Three colour schemes, special trim. Priced at £5,695 with

1,000 for the UK and different derivatives for overseas.

Monte Carlo (Mini-Cooper 1.3i): Rally dress-up kit, four driving lamps, Gunmetal alloy wheels, 165/60-12in tyres, special interior including Mayfair-style wooden facia. Cost £7,995 with 200 cars built for UK.

Cooper Grand Prix (Mini-Cooper 1.3i): Special 86bhp engine, four driving lamps, special 12in alloys with 165-section tyres. Special interior trim. Priced at £13,495 but only 35 cars built to individual order at John Cooper Garages.

Below: The Mini 35SE special edition dated from 1994 – and is backed here by 'Old Number One' of 1959.

Above: Mini Tahiti was another special edition car, first shown in October 1993.

Left: Thirty five years separated 'Old Number One' (621 AOK) and the 35th anniversary car posed alongside it at Gaydon. Nice matching number plates – and very little style change after all that time.

Right: The Mini-Cooper Monte Carlo limited edition was introduced in 1994, to celebrate 30 years since Paddy Hopkirk's famous victory. In the background are the 1964 Monte winner (carrying '37' on the doors) and the 1994 Monte-competing car.

Far right: The Mini Sidewalk limited edition of 1995 was based on the existing Sprite.

Specifications: Mini-Cooper 1990–1996

ENGINE

Description
In-line four-cylinder with cast iron block and cylinder head. Chain-driven camshaft in block, pushrod-operated overhead valves. Heart-shaped combustion chambers. Aluminium alloy pistons, forged steel connecting rods. Three-bearing counter-weighted crankshaft

Capacity
1,275cc (77.8cu in)

Bore and stroke
70.64mm x 81.33mm (2.78in x 3.20in)

Compression ratio
Carburettor 10.5:1, fuel injection 10.0:1

Maximum power
Carburettor 61bhp @ 5,500rpm
Fuel injection 63bhp @ 5,700rpm

Maximum torque
Carburettor 61lb ft (82Nm) @ 3,000rpm
Fuel injection 70lb ft (95Nm) @ 3,900rpm

Fuelling
Single 1½in SU carburettor or Rover single-point fuel injection

TRANSMISSION

Gearbox
Four-speed all synchromesh

Ratios
1st	3.647:1
2nd	2.185:1
3rd	1.425:1
Top	1.000:1
Reverse	3.667:1

Clutch
Borg and Beck, 7⅛in diaphragm spring

Final drive
Helical spur gears, ratio: 3.11:1

BRAKES

Front
Lockheed disc, 8.4in

Rear
Lockheed drum, 7in x 1¼in

Operation
Lockheed hydraulic, vacuum servo

Handbrake
Lever, with cable linkage to rear drums

SUSPENSION

Front
Independent, rubber cone springs, double wishbones, telescopic dampers

Rear
Independent, rubber cone springs, trailing arms, telescopic dampers

STEERING

Type
Rack and pinion

Number of turns lock to lock
2⅛

Turning circle
32ft 0in (9.75m) approx, between kerbs

Steering wheel
Two-spoke, 15¾in diameter

WHEELS AND TYRES
4½J x 12in cast alloy wheels

Tyres
165/60-12in radial-ply (1.3i 145/70-12in, then 165/60-12in from 1995)

PERFORMANCE

Top speed
Carb 87mph (140kph)
1.3i 92mph (148kph)

Acceleration
0–60mph (96kph)   Carb 12.2sec
                  1.3i 11.5sec

Fuel consumption
Carb 33.0mpg (8.6l/100km)
1.3i 32.0mpg (8.8l/100km)

DIMENSIONS

Length
10ft 0¼in (3,054mm)

Width
4ft 7½in (1,410mm)

Height
4ft 5in (1,346mm)

Wheelbase
6ft 8½in (2,036mm)

Track
Front: 3ft 11½in (1,207mm)
Rear: 3ft 10¾in (1,176mm)

Ground Clearance
6.0in (152mm)

Unladen weight
1,535lb (696kg)

1995 Sidewalk (Sprite): Three colour schemes. Sold for £5,895 with 1,000 built for UK.
Cooper S (Mini-Cooper 1.3i): special edition, by John Cooper Garages, though officially approved. With 86bhp engine (as Grand Prix) and engine oil cooler.

Walnut-trimmed facia. Cost was £9,975 but numbers built were not revealed.
1996 EquinoX (Sprite): Three colour schemes. Cost £6,195 with 750 built for UK. Cooper 35 (Mini-Cooper) Three colour schemes, unique interior trim. Gunmetal grey wheels and 165/60-12in tyres. Wooden

facia with cream-faced dials. Priced at £8,195 with 200 produced.
Even after 37 years, though, this was not the end of the story, for between 1998 and 2000 a further eight special editions would appear on the final derivative of the Mini: these are listed in the next chapter.

1996–2000
The final makeover

No sooner had BMW taken control of the Rover Group in 1994 than the German company made a study of all the company's brands. To its astonishment, it discovered that Rover had virtually abandoned the Mini brand to its fate, especially as there was a lack of investment capital to rejuvenate, or replace, the existing models.

Before 1994, Rover's policy was to keep the existing Mini going just as long as there were people to buy it and while the existing specification could meet the legislative requirements of countries in which it was still on sale. BMW, which apparently identified the Mini brand as priceless (to be rated at the same level as other icons such as Coca Cola, McDonald's, or Nike), had other ideas for the future of the marque.

BMW's strategy for the Mini

The situation when BMW took over was explained to me by Rover engineer Chris Lee (who became Project Leader of the replacement Mini): 'It became quite amusing to see just how many people there were who had drawn up a product plan showing the demise of the Mini. And then when it got there, no one had the courage actually to go through with it...

'But...we'd always thought that the Mini was very interesting but we'd never really had our eyes opened to what a powerful brand it actually was...

'When they asked us about the Mini, they were pretty horrified when we said: "When we can't keep it legal, we're going to let it run down."'

BMW marketing expert Torsten Muller-Oetvoes then told me: 'No one at Rover appeared to have a feeling for how valuable the Mini brand could be for them. There was no emotion there...'

It was almost from that moment that BMW decided on a strategy that would revive the fortunes of the Mini. There would be two interrelated strands. Not only would work go ahead at Longbridge to generate an all-new Mini (which BMW would eventually call MINI and appear in 2000) but in the interim, the existing 'classic' type would be given one final, substantial, makeover.

In the next two years, Rover was encouraged to have a good, long, look at the Mini and to bring forward a package of low-investment improvements, which had already been schemed up and tested. Although there was no question of the basic style being updated (not, as the industry might say, in 'sheet-metal' terms at any rate) but all manner of engine, mechanical, and interior trim changes could be considered. Once again, because of its age as a long-running model, the latest Mini did not have to pass the latest stringent barrier crash tests, which it would surely have failed – Rover engineers were very relieved to know of the continuing exemption.

The result was a thoroughly updated Mini, which went on sale in October 1996 and kept the famous old model alive for

another four years. Just 65,695 such cars would be built, many of them being exported, particularly to Japan.

Placarded as having the: 'most radical package of improvements for 36 years' (which was hype but not unacceptably so...), the new type was marketed only as a Mini, Mini-Cooper, or Mini-Cooper with the optional Sport Pack – the last of the previous Sprite and Mayfair saloons had disappeared in August 1996. The unsuccessful Cabriolet, too, was dropped.

New here, new there...

Although the Mini style was not changed – it retained the wide-wheelarch shape, which had become so familiar – there was one important, but hidden, update. For the first-ever time on a Mini, side-impact beams were fitted inside the doors. These useful safety additions were also allied to a steering wheel (actually it was ex-MGF) which had an air bag installed, while the seatbelts had pre-tensioners.

Above: In its 40th anniversary year, BMW couldn't resist setting a lamped-up Mini-Cooper in a snowy scene.

Opposite: As London traffic continued to build up in the 1990s, late-model Minis were nippy enough to get through almost any gaps.

Opposite: The interior of the final-specification Mini, with its Balmoral trim, made a brave show in 1997.

Below: Forty years on, and still in production, the basic Mini poses against London's Millennium Dome in 2000.

This safety package meant that the latest car met European ECD2 regulations and Rover made it clear that the revised car could therefore carry on until 2003 – if the demand was still there.

Under the bonnet there were yet more updates. The familiar 1,275cc engine was henceforth to be fitted with dual-point fuel injection (one injector for each of the siamesed inlet ports), while the distributor had been eliminated in favour of a Rover MEMS2J electronic engine management system. By this time, of course, the compression ratio had been pushed up to 10.5:1 but peak power was still just 63bhp, though now at 5,000rpm.

One bonus connected with multi-point injection was that peak torque was now developed at only 3,000rpm (it had been developed at 3,900rpm on the previous model) and this allowed a much higher final drive ratio (2.76:1) to be specified. The good news was that high-speed cruising was more relaxed and economical than before but the bad news was the little car's acceleration was not up to the standards of the previous model.

From this point, incidentally, automatic transmission was no longer available – not only because it would not have been credible with such high gearing but because demand for this neat and compact four-speed system had been eroding for some years. AP had apparently called Rover's bluff, pointing out that it could not continue providing automatic boxes in such tiny quantities and asking for a guarantee of greater demand.

Visually, too, there was another important change under the bonnet: the water-cooling radiator had finally been moved to the front of the engine bay, instead of living in the left-side inner wheelarch. Mini-watchers had seen front-radiator prototypes running around at Longbridge for at least 20 years but it was not until the need to reduce noise levels arose (new drive-by regulations set a limit of only 74dB instead of 77dB, which doesn't sound much but actually meant halving noise levels) that the radiator move happened.

The new aluminium radiator, plus an electric cooling fan, cooling hoses, and a separate plastic expansion tank, cost considerably more than the old-type radiator (which was retained for cars to be sent to Japan where the new regulations did not apply) but certainly did a great job. The familiar whirring noise of multi-blade side-mounted fans was henceforth banished to the nostalgia cupboard – and the electric fan only cut in when water temperatures rose above a high, preset, level.

The use of a larger, 65 Amp, alternator, was quite obvious, along with the latest type of poly-vee-belt drive for that and the water pump while, out of sight, but equally important in this comprehensive update, was an enhanced catalytic converter and an extra rear silencer box.

Except that a new type of 'pepper-pot' alloy wheel became standard even on the basic (non-Cooper) model – Minilite-style wheels were still standard on Cooper types – the suspension and chassis settings were much as before. When the Sport Pack was specified, 175/50 tyres on 6in-rim 13in Minilite-style alloys were fitted.

Interior revisions

The most obvious improvements were to what an estate agent might call 'fixtures and fittings', for here was a car which had received a complete interior makeover – though the steering wheel was still at the traditional 'drivers need to be alert' angle which Alec Issigonis had specified all those years ago. A truly stylish facia (wood on the Mini-Cooper) was dominated by the MGF-type steering wheel (complete with built-in air bag), the seating was improved, the steering column was now collapsible, and had new control stalks. There was chrome around the instrument bezels and on the door furniture, Balmoral cloth trim on standard cars, and an optional leather interior pack.

Because motoring fashions had changed so much since Alec Issigonis had invented the stripped-to-basics Mini in the 1950s, now there was to be far more opportunity for a buyer to customise his or her new Mini. From the relaunch in October 1996, no fewer than 37 personalizing accessories were available: some as comprehensive as the £795 Sport Pack for Mini-Coopers, some as simple and stand-alone as a wood or alloy gear-lever knob.

Hidden away was a lot more sound-deadening material than ever before, a full state-of-the-art alarm system/engine immobiliser (yes indeed, low-life still liked to steal Minis, especially those with loads of options...), a foam-backed headliner, and a moulded one-piece floor carpet. In a nod towards modern times, too, there was even an intermittent setting for the wipers, and two speeds to the heater fan!

Along with a new range of exterior colours (some of them new, retro-style, which harked back to the 1960s) this sort of makeover, naturally, came at a price, for both the entry-level Mini and Mini-Cooper were priced at £8,995 (the last of the Sprites had cost a mere £6,486, the last of the previous-type Mini-Coopers £8,386) – this certainly accounted for the rather muted response gained by the new models.

It was, of course, easy to pump up those showroom 'sticker' prices by specifying some of the accessories. The Sport Pack (available on Mini-Cooper), at £795, included 13in wheels, fat 175-section radial-ply tyres, extended wheelarch mouldings, Koni dampers, large-bore chrome exhaust tailpipe, an array of four driving/fog lamps, and additional gauges. There were two 'Exterior Bright Accessories Pack' options, one could specify an electrically operated fold-back canvas sunroof, leather upholstery was available, as was a turned alloy facia panel instead of wood, and more, and more...

In so many ways, this was a Mini that had moved up several classes from the original type. No longer a stripped-out, budget-priced, front-wheel-drive runabout, this had instead become the best Mini-based car that the engineers and marketing staffs could put on sale.

What the press thought of the new Mini

It was asking a lot for modern whiz-bang journalist/testers to be kind to the Mini when it had been around for so long. When *Autocar* tested a Mini-Cooper in 1997, the testers felt able only to award it three (out of five) stars and described it as having: 'Prehistoric dynamics, but still great fun'. This test also showed how easy it was to bulk up the price, for this car also featured the £800 Sport Pack, a £500 leather interior, and £265-worth of pearlescent paint. With the standard 63bhp engine, it proved to be capable of just 88mph, with 0–60mph acceleration in 13.3sec – both those figures being slightly down on the factory's own claims.

Even so, the testers discovered that: 'As ever there's a bouncy ride from the all-round independent suspension...but find a smooth, sweeping corner and suddenly it makes sense. Four-wheel-drifts are unheard of in contemporary front-wheel-drive cars, but the Mini is fabulous at pulling them off. Thanks to those tyres [175/50-13in Sport Pack, of course], the Cooper will round corners at perplexingly high speeds with an intimate, if crude, feel through the steering.'

On the other hand, the new marketing approach had not gone unnoticed: 'Today the Mini is even more of a fashion statement than it was in the '60s. Rover admits as much and is set to exploit this with a mesmerising list of options...

'In strictly objective terms the Mini has to be written off as a car from another era. But as an object of basic desire it's still up there with the best of them.'

Above: Nice registration – actually that used by Mike Cooper on his own personal machines in recent years – on the final-model Mini-Cooper of the late 1990s.

Special editions: all based on 1,275cc models

By 1996 Rover was committed to producing regular special edition models to bolster demand for the Mini during quiet periods. Although there was no such car in 1997, the Paul Smith (fashion designer) special arrived in 1998 to revive those traditions: all-in-all there would be seven individually equipped Minis and Mini-Coopers produced before the Mini was finally laid to rest:

Right: Rover produced a flood of special limited edition Minis during the 1990s, this being linked to the fashion model Kate Moss.

1998 Paul Smith (Mini): Dress-up kit, mechanically standard. Charcoal Minilite alloys, colour-coded wheelarch extensions, four driving lamps, and black leather upholstery. Priced at £10,225 with 300 for UK and 1,500 for Japan.

Cooper Sports (Mini-Cooper): Sports suspension package, 6in-rim alloy wheels of 13in diameter, extra wide body-colour wheelarch extensions, and two auxiliary

lamps. Brooklands Green or black, with green leather interior. Sold for £10,525 with 100 cars made.

1999 Cooper S Touring (Mini-Cooper): Available only from John Cooper Garages, with 86bhp engine conversion, suspension upgrade, and 165-section tyres but standard transmission. Special paint job, walnut dashboard, alloy door furniture. £11,595, plus £400 extra for Sports Pack and £1,655 extra for Jack Knight five-speed gearbox.

Cooper S Sport 5 (Mini-Cooper): On sale privately from 1997, officially approved from early 1999. As the Cooper S Touring (above), with Jack Knight five-speed transmission as standard. Rover Sport Pack (13in x 6in alloys, 175/50-section tyres, uprated suspension, extra-wide wheelarch extensions) standard. Leather upholstery and electric sunroof optional extras. Cost £13,650.

Cooper S Works (Mini-Cooper): A JCG conversion, officially approved by Rover. The ultimate in road-going late-model Minis with 90bhp engine, wider tyres on standard wheels (13in wheels as extras), and Jack Knight five-speed gearbox optional. Specially trimmed interior, including alloy dash and door cappings,

lus leather steering wheel. Priced at 12,495 (four-speed), or £14,595 (five-speed) ith 250 cars built.

Mini 40 (Mini): To celebrate 40 years in roduction. Body-colour wheelarch xtensions, twin driving lamps, colour-eyed leather seats, alloy facia, CD player. land Blue, Mulberry Red or Old English White paintwork. Cost £10,995 with 250 or sale in UK.

John Cooper (Mini-Cooper): Mechanically standard but with 13in wheels, specially trimmed/furnished, with extended wheelarches, two driving lamps, leather upholstery, alloy facia, other features, in Brooklands Green with Old English White roof and stripes. Priced at £10,995 with 300 produced, this being the very last factory-supported special edition of all.

2000 Four special run-out models appeared in April 2000 to signal the final wind-down: Classic Seven (£9,495), Classic Cooper (£9,895), and Classic Cooper Sport (£10,895) for the UK, plus the Knightsbridge for European sale only. These were all dress-up jobs with no mechanical innovation or updates.

Classic Seven: Meant to reflect the original Austin Seven of 1959, this was

Below left: The Knightsbridge special edition model of 2000, complete with wide wheelarches and wide-rim alloy wheels, looks intriguing in this night shot.

Below: Nearly there – the Mini-Cooper came to the end of its illustrious career in 2000. This is the final edition Cooper S.

Right: The final edition Mini Seven, manufactured in 2000 just before assembly closed down at Longbridge.

only sold in Old English White, Solar Red, or black and had seat fabrics in grey and red.

Classic Cooper: Very close to the otherwise standard Cooper specification, this car was available in Solar Red, black, British Racing Green, or Tahiti Blue, all with white roof panels. Cloth seats were trimmed in black-and-silver.

Cooper Sport: Complete with the usual Sport Pack, including four driving lamps, this version had the same colour choice as the Cooper, except that Anthracite (grey) replaced black. Seat design was unique, in black and nickel leather, allied to an alloy-finish facia and door cappings.

First and last: changes over 41 years

Feature	Mini 850 1959	Mini-Cooper 2000
Engine	848cc	1,275cc
Power (bhp @ rpm)	34 @ 5,500	63 @ 5,500
Unladen weight	1,380lb	1,576lb
Top speed	75mph	90mph
0–60mph	29.7sec	12.2sec
Price in UK	£497	£9,495

Right: The limited edition Mini-Cooper Sport of 2000 – one of the last of all – featured this startlingly detailed facia layout and style.

The final Rover Minis

Well before the end of the Century, it was clear that the classic Mini was now living on borrowed time. In spite of the lavish launch of October 1996, annual sales had continued to slip – from 16,938 in 1997, to 14,311 in 1998, and to 11,738 in 1999: in every case, far more were going for export (Japan in particular) and less than half stayed in the UK. Not only that but Rover's current owners, BMW, had previewed the all-new next-generation MINI at the Frankfurt Motor Show in September 1997, let it be known that it would go on sale in 2000, and that the classic Mini would finally be dropped to make way for it.

With the new MINI in mind, BMW was clearing the decks at Longbridge. First of all, the Metro was dropped at the end of 1998 so that MINI bodyshell tooling could be installed in the West Works in its place and all technical work on the existing Mini came to an end. When the Mini celebrated its 40th birthday at Silverstone in August 1999, the new MINI made a brief and fleeting appearance too. To balance this, though, the classic Mini was voted European Car of the Century – finishing ahead of other icons such as the VW Beetle.

The fact that BMW walked away from Rover in March 2000 (subsequently selling the company to John Towers's Phoenix consortium for just £10) and that all MINI activity was subsequently transferred to BMW's Cowley (renamed BMW Oxford) plant, made little difference to this process. Even then, with plans to transfer Rover 75 assembly from Cowley to Longbridge beginning to complicate the factory planning process, the Mini was finally doomed.

Signalled weeks in advance, the end finally came on the morning of Wednesday 4 October 2000, when the last Mini of all – a Cooper Sport in Coral red with a white roof – was ceremonially driven off the final assembly line by singer and pop star Lulu. It carried the number plate '1959–2000'. Managing Director Kevin Howe made much of the occasion ('We're paying tribute to a

Left: By 2000, when this very late-model car was built, the Mini's rump must have become one of the most familiar, and best loved, on the planet.

motoring legend, and it's not without a tear in our eye...'), which was also stage managed to show that the Rover 75 was about to start production at Longbridge.

In spite of the hype surrounding the demise of this appealing little car, there was no doubt that its time had come, as sales had almost dried up. Even after a price reduction of about £900, it took time for the last 2,000 stock Minis to find retail customers. In the meantime, BMW had previewed its own all-new MINI,

Left: Although sales had dropped off to only a trickle, the Mini was still a much-loved icon by the time its career came to an end in October 2000.

though sales were not likely to begin until mid-2001.

Now there was no going back and no possibility of revival. Rover announced that no fewer than 5,378,776 Minis of all types had been built since 1959 and that this, the last car of all, would eventually be handed over to the British Motor Industry Heritage Trust at Gaydon, for safe-keeping.

That car, finally registered X411 JOP, went to Gaydon in December 2000 – the handing-over-of-keys ceremony was made with the last car alongside the oldest surviving Morris Mini-Minor of all (621 AOK, originally built on 8 May 1959) – and it now lives in a glass case on the floor of the BMIHT's museum.

This, though, was not the end. To quote Winston Churchill, after the triumph of the battle of Alamein in 1942: 'This is not the end. It is not even the beginning of the end. But it is, perhaps, the end of the beginning...' Although new-car assembly had ended, the Mini's reputation continued to grow. Every time the new MINI made the news, a damp-eyed writer would invariably refer to the original car. Mini one-makers continued to grow, as did the restoration business, which followed up.

The best possible news for classic Mini enthusiasts was that the old production line machinery – in particular, the press

Right: To give the classic Mini a high-profile send-off, Rover asked Lulu to greet the very last car as it was built.

Far right: The very last Mini, a Mini-Cooper so characteristically painted in red with the white roof, was built in October 2000. Pop star Lulu drove the car off the line, Rover CEO Kevin Howe (far left) watched it arrive, and the new-generation Rover 75 (behind Howe) was ready to take over.

Right: After production of the classic Mini ended in October 2000, MG Rover handed it over to the British Motor Industry Heritage Trust, for permanent exhibition at Gaydon. In the handover ceremony Bob Dover (Chairman and CEO of BMIHT and Land Rover) shakes hands with Nick Stephenson (Deputy Chairman of MG Rover). 'Old Number One' – the Morris-badged Mini built in the spring of 1959 – is posing in the same group.

Opposite: The last classic Mini of all was produced, at Longbridge, in October 2000.

tools and fixtures – was eventually handed over from Longbridge to the British Motor Heritage enterprise at Witney, near Oxford, which ensured a long-term supply of parts, panels, and – eventually – complete bodyshells.

When the Mini was finally laid to rest, most of the design team had gone ahead but Jack Daniels (Alec Issigonis's faithful interpreter and 'pencil man') was still alive, mentally alert at 88 years of age,

and proud to recall some of the highlights of this fabulous machine's career: 'I'm both proud and sad. I never thought the car would last 41 years, but everyone has had one, from royalty downwards...'

Perhaps it was as well that BMW's new-generation MINI bore no technical relationship to the classic Mini, for Alec Issigonis would have hated that. Quite simply, his Mini was irreplaceable...

Mini production milestones

First production car	April 1959
Millionth car	February 1965
Two millionth car	May 1969
Three millionth car	December 1972
Four millionth car	November 1976
Five millionth car	February 1986
Last car of all	October 2000

Cancelled Mini projects

Replacing a car as famous as the original Mini was always going to be difficult. Time and again, resourceful and inventive engineers and planners would dabble, sketch and sometimes even build a prototype, but until BMW came on the scene in the mid-1990s they never made it into the showrooms.

Reason? The most important, no question, was that the original car was so outstanding that it would take a miracle to develop something which was better. Then, if the style and technical improvements could be delivered, there was the cost of putting it into production. Not least, too, was the fact that Minis never made much of a profit, so the money-men could always think of a better way of investing in British Leyland's future.

Right: Look carefully and you will realise that this is no ordinary Mini. During the 1970s, Sir Alec Issigonis's tiny development team developed the 'gearless Mini', with an overhead-camshaft engine and a prototype automatic transmission.

9X: Mini, the second time around

When Alec Issigonis set out to renew the entire BMC product range in the late 1960s, a new Mini was his first priority. Many Issigonis-watchers found this inevitable. One of his closest associates told me: 'The Mini was his one "great idea", and he wanted to be remembered for it. Every other BMC car which followed was bigger, heavier and somehow less "pure". He wasn't really interested in them. He only really enjoyed working on Minis...'

In 1967, therefore, and with just six hand-picked engineers, in self-contained workshops, he finally set out to produce a Mini-replacement. This was 9X, the first of several 'pie-in-the-sky' schemes that spluttered into life over the years.

Issigonis decided that 9X was to have a new structure, new engine, and new suspension. His target was to make 9X smaller, lighter, and at least five per cent cheaper to build than the existing Mini.

with Jaguar) merged with Leyland in 1968, to form British Leyland. When British Leyland's hierarchy walked into Longbridge in May 1968, they could find no sign of Issigonis in the main engineering department. When eventually discovered, his new Mini was at once assessed, his engine master plan was abandoned, and all impetus behind 9X was lost.

For Issigonis, the capital costs required never seemed to be an issue. For British Leyland, once it had seen the new car that had been designed, it became the only issue.

Although the first 9X was completed in 1968/1969, little testing ever took place. Harry Webster (ex-Standard-Triumph technical chief) took over as Technical Director of the newly named Austin-Morris Division in May 1968. Although orders went out for 9X to be scrapped, Issigonis and his loyal associates, made sure that the hardware was stored away instead and preserved. (One car survived and was later handed over to the British Motor Heritage Trust at Gaydon.) Soon after this Alec Issigonis was finally sidelined, given the rather nebulous title of Director of Research and Development, and never again influenced mainstream design at Longbridge.

Left: One of Sir Alec Issigonis's final projects was to link the 9X-type overhead-camshaft engine to a new type of 'gearless' fully automatic transmission. This led to the building of a 'gearless Mini' prototype, which survives to this day.

Below: If Alec Issigonis had got his way, by the 1970s the Mini would have moved on into a second-generation model, which was coded 9X. In 1968, this was the single-overhead-camshaft engine proposed for that car, whose engine bay was even smaller than the original.

With no limits yet set on capital spending, or on technological innovation, this was an audacious target.

The structure was new, with sharper and more angular lines. There were no exposed body seams. Proportions were fresh and crisp and the bonnet was extremely short. Because it was wider, at 58½in, the cabin was slightly larger than that of the Mini. There was more glass and a new type of 'half-hatchback' feature, with a lift-up rear window. Issigonis had personally approved the style, though the shape was certainly influenced by BMC's favoured consultant, Pininfarina. Although 9X was 4in shorter than the Mini, its wheelbase was 4in longer. This meant that the cabin was longer, with a better driving position. There was no sign of the Mini's original bulky subframes and the suspension was by conventional steel springs – MacPherson struts at the front and transverse torsion bars at the rear.

The 43bhp 850cc engine, though, was the first of a proposed new family: four or six cylinders, 750cc to 1,300cc, all with aluminium heads, cast-iron blocks, single overhead camshaft/cogged belt drive valve gear, and two valves per cylinder.

The electric alternator was built into the main mass of the flywheel and the transmission (still under the engine, rather than end-on) was a simpler two-shaft design. This astonishing little power unit was 25 per cent more efficient than the A-series and, complete with transmission, weighed only 200lb: this was a 40 per cent reduction on the A-series pack, which weighed 340lb. A stretch to 1,000cc was feasible. The new engine was so small, and the 9X engine bay built so cosily round it, that prototype cars could not possibly have run with A-series engines instead. That, in a way, was the project's eventual undoing.

Two 9X prototypes were completed, then sidelined: astonishingly, the programme was not formally abandoned until 1977. Unhappily for Issigonis, it evolved at the same time as BMH (BMC had joined forces

Early 1970s Mini replacements

From late 1972 to early 1974, in parallel with ADO74 (which I describe next), studies were made for a 'Classic Mini replacement', which would have used an existing Mini platform – with either an 80in (saloon) or 84in (estate car) wheelbase – with a new three-door body style. Seven different stages of development were studied, the schemes gradually growing from 120in to 125in overall length and from 55.9in to 59in wide.

New outer skin panels would have been used (this was a classic reskin), to include curved side glasses, both for doors and rear quarter windows, all to provide a more generous interior package.

All schemes retained the existing Mini A-series engine/transmission layout but with a front-mounted radiator. Initially existing Mini subframes were retained but later schemes used ADO67/Austin Allegro rear suspension instead.

No prototypes were actually built.

ADO74: a larger Mini

The next full-scale attempt to replace the Mini came in the early 1970s. Coded ADO74, this project was always envisaged as a slightly larger car, to replace the latest long-nose Minis – the Mini Clubman and 1275GT types.

From June 1972 to March 1974, much styling and engineering effort was expended. Intended to use a brand-new overhead camshaft K-series engine (not the same K-series that eventually went on sale at the end of the 1980s, for this had evolved from the earlier H-series), prototype engines ran for 25,000 road-test miles and 800 test-bed hours.

ADO74 was larger, even, than the long-nosed Mini Clubman. In this design the eight-valve/overhead-camshaft K-series would have been of 1,100cc or 1,300cc, transversely mounted, and steeply inclined back towards the passenger bulkhead, with a five-speed transmission behind it. The new car was to have an 88in wheelbase, with MacPherson strut front suspension and coil spring independent rear suspension.

ADO74 progressed as far as styling clays and package drawings: a single bare bodyshell was built. A style theme was already chosen and engineering development was about to begin when, in March 1974, it was discovered that £130 million would be needed to get the new car and the new engine into production – this was money that British Leyland did not have, so a decision was made to cancel the project.

A comparison of ADO74, with the short-nose Mini

Feature	ADO74	Classic Mini
Length	138in	120¼in
Wheelbase	88in	80⅖in
Width	61½in	55in
Height	52in	53in
Front track	52in	47⅜in
Rear track	52in	45⅝in
Wheel diameter	12in	10in

Overhead-camshaft conversions of existing engines

A-series: To minimise the cost of new engine investment, single-overhead-camshaft conversions of the ageing A-series power unit were developed in the mid-1970s. These featured simple, vertical, eight-valve layouts, the cylinder heads being aluminium, with camshaft drive by internally cogged belt.

Three engine sizes – 970cc, 1,097cc and 1,275cc – were proposed and developed in prototype form, the test bed power being 59bhp (970cc) to 84bhp (1,275cc). No fewer than 2,000 test-bed hours were completed, along with 2,200 miles in various test cars.

Three-cylinder E-series: The conventional four-cylinder E-series was an overhead-camshaft type being used in Austin Maxi (from 1969) and Allegro (from 1973) models, with slightly inclined inlet and exhaust valves, driven via fingers. With improved packaging and lighter weight in mind, three-cylinder varieties were investigated in 1975 – a 1,750cc 'four' therefore becoming a 1,300cc 'three'.

Studies showed that 970cc and 1,300cc three-cylinder engines could certainly have been refined and would have been short enough to have mated with the desired end-on gearbox in a new model.

Unhappily, these modified versions of existing engines did not appeal, and were abandoned.

Mini Metro

Launched in 1980, re-badged as a Rover in 1994, and finally dropped at the end of 199 this was the first 'Mini replacement' to go o sale – yet the Issigonis Mini outlived it.

Soon after ADO74 was cancelled, work o a successor began. This time, though, it hac to retain the existing engine/transmission. With Charles Griffin now in overall technical command of such projects, the new ADO88 got under way. Griffin's brief was that ADO88 should be a little longer than the long-nose Mini Clubman. With an 88in wheelbase, it was to be a three-door hatchback, with the most spacious possible interior seating package. When it went on sale, it was 134in long, a full 14in longer than the classic Mini.

For a long time, its launch date was planned for October 1978, this eventually slipping to 1979. The original style changed little over the years – until in 1977/1978 a new management change caused the style to be made more bulbous, when it became LC8.

Although it was to re-use existing Mini power trains (A-series engines, with a choice of manual or automatic transmissions), rubber cone and Hydrolastic suspensions were both discarded in favour of the new Hydragas system.

After the style was approved in February 1976, 34 prototypes had been built before a British Leyland management upheaval saw Sir Michael Edwardes become Chief Executive. An early decision was to have the ADO88 style revised. Without incurring huge financial penalties (tooling of many major body panels had already begun), a complete reskin exercise was completed – in a mere six weeks. In the process, ADO88 became LC8 and the public launch was set for October 1980.

At this point, management decided that the LC8/'Mighty Mini' should not replace every Mini after all. Because the classic Mini was still selling at 200,000 cars a year, it was decided to keep it going. 'Mighty Mini' (soon to be christened Mini Metro) would be assembled at Longbridge, would replace the Mini Clubman/1275GT types, and would carve out its own niche.

New body manufacturing facilities were erected at West Works, shell delivery was arranged by overhead conveyors, and new assembly lines were prepared, to accommodate up to 6,500 cars every week. Once the Mini Metro started to roll, more than £300 million had been spent (more than ADO74 would have cost) but in the meantime rampant inflation had made a nonsense of comparisons.

The Mini Metro gamble worked well. By 1981 the revamped Longbridge plant was already producing 3,000 Metros every week and this would eventually be eased up to 4,500.

Yet the old dilemma – how to replace the Mini – remained. The Metro was an enduring success but could not replace the Mini itself: as a result, combined sales shot up. In 1979, 165,500 classic Minis had been built but in 1981 no fewer than 235,750

Metros and Minis were produced, the trends still being upwards.

Inevitably, the Metro took many sales away from the Mini. Both cars sat, side by side, in British Leyland showrooms and customers had to make a choice. Did they want a classic Mini – cheap, small, cheeky, nippy, but beginning to look old-fashioned? Or did they want a Metro, less sporty in character and inevitably more expensive but more roomy, with a practical hatchback feature, and a higher-quality and more versatile interior?

To widen the gap, Rover (the company name that finally emerged from the wreckage of British Leyland/BL/Austin-Rover) elected to move the Metro upmarket. By

revamping the front-end structure (notably by widening the engine bay and the chassis 'legs' which embraced it), it became possible to insert the Rover 200's new overhead-camshaft K-series engine, complete with R65 transmission – instead of the ancient A-series power unit. Although British prices therefore rocketed (in 1990 A-series engined cars spanned £5,575–£7,765, whereas the new K-Series engined cars cost £5,985–£9,735), these were significantly better cars, which felt altogether more mature.

That progress was carried on further (and finally) in December 1994, when, under BMW's tutelage, the Metro was facelifted and renamed Rover 100, which is how it ended its career in 1998.

Mini and Mini Metro: a 1980/1981 comparison

Feature	Mini	Mini Metro
	1000 Super	(998cc)
Layout	2-door saloon	3-door hatchback
Engine size	998cc	998cc
Power (bhp @ rpm)	39 @ 4,750	44 @ 5,250
Overall length	10ft 0¼in	11ft 2in
Overall width	4ft 7in	5ft 0⅝in
Wheelbase	6ft 8½in	7ft 4⅜in
Weight	1,375lb	1,638lb
Top Speed	82mph	84mph
0–60mph	18.7sec	18.9sec
Price in UK	£3,031	£3,095

Left: The Mini Metro, launched in October 1980, had been intended to replace the Mini but did not do so and ultimately the Mini outlived it.

Postscript

When the classic Mini finally dropped out of production in October 2000, there was never any danger that it would be forgotten. Well before then (and particularly after the 'Cooper' badge had been reintroduced), the brand had become immortal, taken on a momentum of its own, and was almost bound to live for ever.

Yet this was a brand, and a range of models, which had been shamelessly neglected throughout the 1970s and 1980s: by the 1990s, when Rover was trying again, it was too late to restore the Mini as a best-seller, but merely to keep it ticking over until the march of time, of new legislative hazards, or of a new model, should nudge it into retirement.

Well before the end, a phalanx of one-make, one-model, or even one-region, clubs had sprung up to service the cars, not only in the UK and Europe, but all over the world. In the UK, by the 2000s not only were there national clubs like the Mini-Cooper Register (a thriving organisation), but there were clubs catering for individual models like the Moke, clubs catering for people who lived within a few miles of a particular town or city, and even for organisations looking after ex-works competition cars.

Some of those clubs were deliberately angled towards motor sport, for though new classic Minis are no longer being made, there is a thriving cottage industry which supports the building of cars for racing, rallycross, auto tests and Historic rallies.

Below: Even in old age, Mini, complete with Minilite-style alloy wheels, looks very smart. Tens of thousands have been preserved into the new century.

No one, therefore, need own a Mini and lack for companionship. Purely as an example, the author called up Google on the internet, keyed in the words 'Mini Clubs', asked the question – and came up with 18,600,000 references. No lack of choice there. As an alternative, all that was needed was to pick up one of the Mini-orientated magazines and look for the Clubs Directories, which are published regularly.

In the UK in 2006, two well-established magazines – *Mini Magazine* and *Mini World* – cater exclusively for this car, while in North America the recently-established *MC Squared* (which covers classic and modern MINI types) rapidly built up its own reputation. Other publications, on other continents, added their own service.

With 5.4 million Minis of all types originally built, there was always a healthy market for spare parts, a situation that the suppliers' computers predicted would continue for years to come. In the 1980s, for sure, there was a developing problem in procuring body panels and trim parts

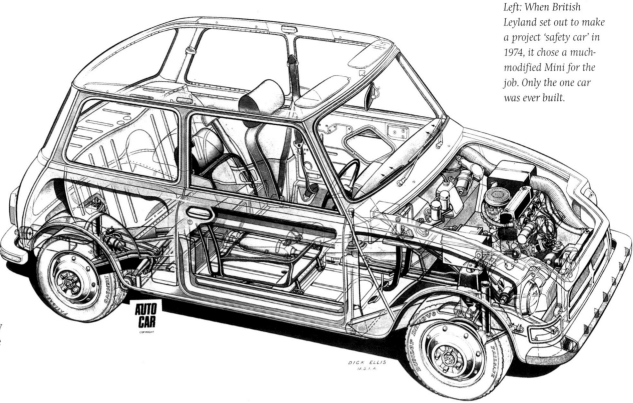

Left: When British Leyland set out to make a project 'safety car' in 1974, it chose a much-modified Mini for the job. Only the one car was ever built.

Left: By 1981, the Mini was about to be swamped by the Metro, but a full range remained on sale, including one of the last of the Clubman-nosed estate cars.

Right: Most Minis had the same snub-nosed style, but over the years there were myriads of colours. This was one of the very last, Mk III, Mini-Cooper 1275S saloons of 1971.

but this process was reversed as the 1990s progressed. In the case of trim parts, with such a significant 'car park' in place, there was a demand for replica or pattern parts, which was soon satisfied.

More recently, in the 2000s, that enterprising organisation, British Motor Heritage (once controlled by BMW but, following a management buy-out, once again an independent organisation), was able to supply new panels from original press tools and even to supply complete bodyshells too.

The supply of A-series engines, engine parts, tune-up expertise, and the transmission of knowledge to go with them is now so enormous that the abiding problem is only one of choice – and confusion for the novice. More than 20 million A-series of all types were built for

Left: In twenty years (1966 to 1986), the shape of Minis – and of pretty girls – changed very little. Did you say something... ?

Above: Restoration of a Mini today is eased by the availability of most replacement steel panels – it is the tiny details, like this false wood strip around Clubman estate rear doors, which may add to the delays.

Left: British Leyland hoped that the Mini Metro would replace the Mini completely, but that never happened. Instead, the two totally different cars co-existed, side-by-side, for nearly 20 years.

Below: Over the years there were several different fascia/dashboard layouts inside Minis. This was the Italian-built Innocenti Mini of the mid-1970s.

BMC and British Leyland models of many types, and more than ten million 'gearbox-in-sump' types, so that shortages are unthinkable.

There is, on the other hand, no scope for further development of engine power, for every possible improvement of that quirky cylinder head, in any of its forms, was made years ago. More recent cocky pronouncements of breakthroughs have invariably proved to be ephemeral.

Traditionalists, at this point, should therefore look elsewhere, for in recent years there has been a growing business in providing engine transplants, more robust and more powerful than the old-type A-series. Some Minis, for sure have more than 200bhp engines but this power invariably comes from other makes, of which small Ford, Honda, and Vauxhall units have all proved effective.

If ever there is a car which deserves to live for ever, then the Mini, in all its forms is it. With the help of the hundreds of thousands of enthusiasts who keep the faith, their dream might, just might, be realised.

Index